Islam and Franciscanism:
A Dialogue

Spirit and Life: A Journal of Contemporary Franciscanism serves as a vehicle for the publication of papers presented at various conferences, symposia, and/or workshops which seek to bring the Franciscan tradition into creative dialogue with contemporary theology, philosophy, spirituality, psychology, and history. The Journal is an occasional publication. During the fiftieth anniversary year of the Franciscan Institute (1991), the publication of this Journal was a refounding of an earlier Franciscan Institute series entitled *Spirit and Life*, established in 1948 by the Rev. Philotheus Boehner, O.F.M., one of the co-founders and first director of The Franciscan Institute.

The papers contained in this volume were originally prepared for a dialogue sponsored by the May-Bonfils Foundation which brought together Christian-Franciscan and Muslim scholars. The papers are published here with the assistance of a grant from the May-Bonfils Foundation.

ISBN 1-57659-169-7

Library of Congress Catalog Card Number:

00-104116

Printed by
BookMasters
Ashland, Ohio

Spirit and Life
A Journal of Contemporary Franciscanism

Volume 9   *2000*

Islam and Franciscanism:
A Dialogue

Series Editor:
Margaret Carney, O.S.F.

Volume Editors:
Daniel Dwyer, O.F.M. and Hugh Hines, O.F.M.

Contents

INTRODUCTION

In recent years the need for understanding between Christians and Muslims has reached a state of urgency. Dialogue between believers in the world's two largest faith traditions can no longer be relegated to antiquarians or to specialists in far–off, and hitherto exotic, places. In the world, and in our European and North American neighborhoods, misunderstanding and tension between Muslims and Christians has often become very visible. Sometimes the results have been tragic. From Bosnia to Indonesia, and from the Netherlands to New Jersey, these two great monotheistic traditions are being brought face to face. It is time that we met as brothers and sisters.

For those Christians who follow St. Francis of Assisi there is an even greater impetus for dialogue. We have, in the life of our founder, one of the earliest examples of peaceful and respectful interaction between Christians and Muslims. In the year 1219 C.E. (597 A.H.), Francis traveled from Italy to Acre and then on to the Egyptian city of Damietta. In the midst of the Crusades he crossed over into "enemy" territory accompanied only by one companion —Brother Illuminato. Amazingly, Francis succeeded in coming face to face with Sultan Melek-el-Kamil; and for several days the two men conversed. According to the sources, they engaged in a respectful and honest exchange, and afterwards Francis was allowed to depart in peace.[1]

Though the event merited barely a footnote in the history of the Crusades, it has assumed fresh importance for the Franciscan movement of our own day. Conscious of this tradition and of the growing number of situations in which Christians and Muslims come in contact, the friars who serve on the board of Holy Name Province's Bonfils Seminar decided to sponsor a dialogue. We hoped to bring together representatives of the Franciscan and Islamic traditions in an atmosphere of trust, congeniality and scholarship. Over the course of several years a small group of believers,

---

[1] John Moorman, *A History of the Franciscan Order* (Chicago, 1988).

sponsored by Holy Name Province and the Mae–Bonfils Trust, gathered at the Giorgio Hotel in Denver, Colorado. Hosted by Frs. Daniel Dwyer, O.F.M. and Hugh Hines, O.F.M. our group consisted of five invited guests—two Muslims and three Franciscan Christians. Out of their conversations and sharing came the articles contained in this volume.

Though the proceedings took place in a pleasant and harmonious context, the discussions that ensued were also very frank and honest. At times it was clear that our knowledge of each other's beliefs and practices was incomplete. On occasion we realized that even our vocabularies were different; yet we came away with a deep respect for our colleagues and for the way in which each person understood and lived his respective tradition. We grew each day in the awareness that we were all sons in faith of Abraham and children of the same God.

It need hardly be stated that these essays are only a beginning, and that our very small gathering represented a tiny step forward. It was particularly regrettable that, due to last minute emergencies, we were unable to have a third Muslim scholar engaged in the process. We were also most cognizant of the fact that ours was an all male group. We hope that future endeavors can expand on what we have accomplished.

Despite our limitations and the limitations of these essays, we came away from this seminar with a real sense of accomplishment and with a renewed interest in each other's traditions. It should be noted that our Muslim scholars had an extra task to some extent. They were not only adding to their knowledge of Christianity but were forced to delve into the less familiar area of Franciscanism. They are to be congratulated for the enthusiasm and spirit that each brought to this task.

The essays presented here are arranged so as to move from the general to the more specific, and from contemplation to action. Each is also quite unique in emphasis.

Imam Mohammad Bashar Arafat, a native of Syria, is the director of AN-NUR Institute and Muslim Chaplain at Johns Hopkins University. He presents us with a work that is very meditative and thoughtful. The Imam issues a heartfelt cry for "deliverance through people of profound integrity and faith working in acquaintance and religious toleration." He reveals a devout Muslim's understanding of the relationship between Christianity and Islam; but he also recognizes the need for common actions in a world that is often very hostile to both of our traditions and to the many values that we hold in common. His essay is one that should speak to the heart of Muslims and Christians. While remaining faithful to his own tradition, the Imam causes us to realize how close we already are in our beliefs and in our desire to worship and serve the one God. His essay exemplifies the spirit that united all the authors when he states:

> I believe our love for God should be like the love shown by Mohammed, Jesus, Moses, Abraham, and all other prophets which resulted in peace, brotherhood, and respect among the 'Global Family of Adam and Eve' regardless of race or color.

Brother François Paquette, OFM is a member of the Franciscan Province of St. Joseph located in Quebec. A resident of Montreal, he is also President of the International Franciscan (OFM) Commission for Relations with the Muslims. His essay is entitled "Breaking Down the Walls of Difference: Islamic—Christian Encounters Through Prayer." His approach is one that brings us to a central element of both of our experiences of prayer. For those who are not familiar with ritual life and practices in either Christianity or Islam, Brother Paquette's essay is most informative. He also brings us to a more specific focus on the Franciscan Tradition. Even committed Catholic Christians may be unfamiliar with Franciscan traditions such as the "Crown," or of the origin of practices such as the Stations of the Cross. Once these practices are adequately explained, Brother Paquette goes on to look at the way in which Muslims and Franciscans have begun to share their spiritual riches with each other. Brother Paquette explains how joint ventures in prayer often coincide with common educational efforts and united actions for justice in areas such as Bosnia and Herzegovina. He rightly points out that we "have the same origin and the same ultimate end..." and he reminds us that "... all respectful and welcome regard for the prayer of another must inevitably lead to a desire to come together to serve the well-being of humanity..."

Dr. Fareed Munir finds himself in a most advantageous situation for a dialogue such as ours. An American and a former Imam, Dr. Munir is currently a Professor on the Religious Studies faculty of Siena College. As a Muslim professor teaching at a Franciscan school, he is necessarily engaged in dialogue each and every day. Dr. Munir's essay is entitled "Islam and Franciscanism: The Prophet Muhammad of Arabia and St. Francis of Assisi in the Spirituality of Mission." In his work Dr. Munir returns to the story that helped to launch our dialogue. He goes back to the visit of St. Francis and Sultan al-Kamil; but he is able to view that story through Muslim eyes. Dr. Munir is then led to compare the position of Francis with that of the Prophet Muhammad, particularly in regard to their respective view of mission. Christians might be surprised to read that the sultan "recognized the Muslim-like character of St. Francis"; and Muslims might be surprised to note that "St. Francis was a good Muslim." These conclusions come out of Dr. Munir's extensive reading in our troubled history. He provides us with some tantalizing new possibilities for further research and for ongoing solidarity.

Just as Dr. Munir finds similarities in our concepts of mission, Fr. Thomas Mooren finds that both traditions share what he calls an "Exodus Motif." That is, both Christians and Muslims know what it is like to "leave behind us at least something of our own self..." as we seek to encounter God/Allah. This, according to Fr. Mooren, was the path of Abraham, the common father of Jews, Christians and Muslims. It was also the path of the Prophet Muhammad and of St. Francis of Assisi. Indeed, Fr. Mooren finds that "the Exodus Motif" is an essential part of most true religious experience. He broadens our viewpoint by finding evidence of it in Buddhism and Taoism as well as in the great monotheistic faiths. He notes too, that this motif was very important in the theology of St. Paul who, in his letter to the Galatians, reminds us of the call that went out to Abraham, the call to "...leave your country and your father's house, for the land that I will show you." (Gen. 12, 1) Fr. Mooren notes that this was, in a sense, the same call that was heeded by the Prophet Muhammad when he embraced true monotheism, and by

St. Francis when he abandoned his earthly father for his heavenly one.

Fr. Mooren himself might be said to have followed the Exodus pattern. A Capuchin Franciscan Friar, he left his native Germany in order to serve as a professor of Mission and Interreligious studies at St. Paul University in Ottawa, Canada. Fr. Mooren has had the advantage of living and working in predominantly Muslim countries such as Egypt and Indonesia.

Another Franciscan with long years of experience in the Islamic world is Fr. Anselm Moons, a Franciscan Friar from the Netherlands. Fr. Moons spent many years living among Muslim peoples in Pakistan, and so he brings a wealth of experience to his scholarly endeavors. He has entitled his essay "The Arrogance of Ownership: Environment and Economy in Religious Focus." Fr. Moons reminds us that good will and mutual esteem are just necessary beginnings in the Christian-Islamic dialogue. Both Muslims and Franciscans must translate their beliefs into common actions for the good of humanity. He reminds us of the "corrosive self interest" that is laying waste our planet, tormenting the poor, and threatening all of God's creation with disaster. He calls us to remember that, for both Muslims and Christians, the greatest offense a person can commit is idolatry. Today, he notes, we are all in danger of worshipping "the idol of Mammon." Fr. Moons's wide ranging essay centers on the issue of property, a concern at the heart of the Franciscan tradition that Moons sees as an essential issue in Islam as well. He notes that Muslims and Christians are faced with the same struggles in every corner of the globe:

> ...they worry about the increasing number of people below the poverty line, the exploitation of women, children, migrant workers, indigenous people ...they also qualify the ecological destruction as an outright offense of the Creator which hurts especially those who have a 'fragile relationship with nature'...

His essay motivates the reader to address issues of ecology and, though he does not minimize the challenges we face, he ends with "rays of hope."

Perhaps our dialogue, remembered in these essays, is itself a small "ray of hope." Those of us who were privileged to gather in Denver gained new friends and a new sense of commitment to our God. We can no longer think of each other's faith tradition without remembering with respect our newfound brothers. May these essays convey some sense of our spirit and may they spark future peaceful endeavors among the children of Abraham.

Daniel P. Dwyer O.F.M.

ISLAM AND CHRISTIANITY
—TWO FAITHS AND ONE GOD—

A Personal Reflection

Imam Mohammad Bashar Arafat, Ph.D.

Preface

The teachings of Islam and Christianity flow from one source, God, The One, The Creator. This paper, which was written for the project **"Islam and Franciscanism"** is meant to create an awareness of the common beliefs and values held by those who believe in Allah — the Arabic name for God. It also emphasizes the duty of the true believers, in our case, Muslims and Christians, clergy and lay people, to stand united as a brick wall against the various forces that are trying to destroy faith and morality and establish a non-religious society naked of any moral values.

Dialogue and continuous meetings between the Muslim and Christian world are more important than ever before, to help prevent the evil forces from interfering and igniting wars under the name of religion. I believe our love for God should be like the love shown by Moḥammad, Jesus, Moses, Abraham, and all other prophets which resulted in peace, brotherhood and respect among the "Global Family of Adam and Eve" regardless of race or color.

When we look at a specific tradition within the Christian faith, Franciscanism and its leader, St. Francis of Assisi, served as an early pioneer attempting to build bridges of understanding. If St. Francis was in this century, the age of religious freedom, tolerance, and openness toward others, I believe his active role in the mission of peace would not have been limited to the Sultan of Egypt. It would have been extended throughout other parts of the Muslim World. Courageous people like

St. Francis and the Sultan of Egypt are needed in each generation to ensure the continuation of the spirit of the divine message brought by Mohammad, Jesus, and all prophets of God.

IN THE NAME OF ALLAH, MOST MERCIFUL, MOST BENEFICENT

WHAT IS ISLAM ABOUT

Islam as a new belief system was introduced to humanity more than fourteen centuries ago, but in actual fact it is a reality with its roots in creation itself. It is the Truth that has accompanied man from his very beginning. Since then, a chain of prophets has been sent to remind man of this Truth. By doing so, man has been linked to his Lord and Creator, Who through His prophets has progressively expanded His message over the millennia.

Islam, which means **"submission to God,"** reflects the relationship between the human being and God that is seen in all religions and in the message of all the messengers of God. Thus, on this point, there can be no conflict between what has been revealed to Moses, Jesus, or Mohammad. The Qur`ān affirms this religious unity and the common prophetic brotherhood of the messengers and condemns their segregation.

> He has ordained for you that religion which He commanded unto Noah, and that which We inspire in you, and that which We commanded unto Abraham and Moses and Jesus, saying: Establish (the religion) and be not divided therein....[1]

Despite differences of time, place, and people, this comprehensive unity which is the religion of God, is founded on a natural disposition cultured by a rational mind and heart. The aptitude of man to live this life and that of the hereafter, find completion within the framework of this rationality.

---

[1] *The Holy Qur`ān*, Sura 42, The Counsel, verse 13. Hereafter *The Holy Qur`ān* is referred to by the abbreviation T.Q.

The teachings of Islam, therefore, aim to protect this disposition and strive to maintain its purity despite the diseases that continuously afflict it. This protection is afforded through a religious education that sees the importance of this natural disposition as the sciences see the universe, in their ability to expand knowledge and the intellect. This religious training purifies and refines man's nature, teaching him to recognize his true purpose and goal. The Qur`ān considers piety the essence of man's nature, like that seen in the lives of the prophets.

The life of Prophet Muhammad represents rejuvenation and not a pioneering struggle, a confirmation and a complement to the work of the earlier prophets. This is because the central theme of Islam revolves around the unity of God, a subject to which the Qur`ān devotes much attention, and the Qur`ān filled with arguments that guide man towards God, teaching him to recognize his Lord and Creator. Its arguments are highly eloquent and enlightening, causing man to be aware of the universe around him and reflect on the lessons it has to give.

Confirmation of the unity of God is the distinguishing feature of Islam. For Muslims, He is Unique, the Sponsor of mankind to Whom hearts turn and with Whom all seek to connect. He is One, without partner, and He is without equal, for He is the Lord of creation. He is the Pre-eternal, Uncreated, neither begetting nor begot, possessing neither spouse nor offspring, neither limited by space or time, nor having any substance. All that exists is His creation, which stands in need of Him. He is the Ultimate sanctuary in times of difficulty.

> The Originator of the heavens and the earth! How can He have a child, when there is for Him no consort, when He created all things and is aware of all things? Such is Allah, your Lord. There is no God save Him, the Creator of all things, so worship Him and He takes care of all things.[2]

The consequences of this monotheistic belief are actions that manifest themselves in the love of the believer for his Lord, a love that binds the believer through reliance and sincerity. Islam demands belief in the Hereafter, where we are rewarded for deeds in this life and our lives continue after this earthly existence. Hence, the futility of the lives of the unbelievers who, despite the pleasure and ease they may find in

---

[2]T.Q., Sura 6, The Cattle, verses 101-102.

their present existence, will eventually discover unhappiness and despair in this life and an eternity of the same in the next. On the other hand, those who pursue this life more seriously with a God-consciousness that directs their deeds and actions toward good meet with the best rewards in the next, although they may be insignificant and subject to disdain from those around them in this life.

> The scale of that day is of justice. As for those whose scale is heavy, they are the successful. And for those whose scale is light, those are they who have wronged their souls because they were of those who wronged our revelations.[3]

Regarding this present world, even a passing glance will show a strong connection between the perfection of faith and a positive outlook on life. Mankind, as understood by Islam, is the Lord of his environment.

> See you not how Allah has made subservient to you whatsoever is in the skies and whatsoever is in the earth and has bestowed upon you of His favors both seen and unseen...[4]

Thus, we see that the Qur`ān connects humanity with the universe by consideration of the myriad spectacles of creation that life has to hold. It ties the material life of man to his actions in that he must struggle in this life for material gain. Similarly, the more aesthetic aspects of life bear fruit in intellectual exercises.

Of course, Islam disagrees with the idea that life is a 'free for all,' having no one to govern it, and that man was created by a mere act of chance, for this philosophy encourages man to squander his life in idle pursuits. Muslims believe that Allah has granted us this life and settled us in this world as a means to know Him. Early Islamic civilizations were founded with this reasoning and sound moral principle. They developed highly cultured societies that brought much good to the world and bequeathed to it a rich heritage.

Islam proclaims freedom of thought, while at the same time limiting the freedom of desires that bring about disorder in society. It concerns itself with the affairs of man both in the present world and the world to come by focusing on the physical and spiritual activities in this

---

[3]T.Q., Sura 7, The Heights, verses 8-9.
[4]T.Q., Sura 31, Luqman, verse 20.

life. This is because Islam sees man as an intricate whole without division and that his desired perfection lies in the successful struggle in both the material and spiritual planes, in a formula that equates success in this world with the everlasting success in the Hereafter. Thus, failure to build a proper foundation will bring about the collapse and eventual destruction of man and his society in this life and eternal despair in the afterlife.

> Whosoever is blind here will be blind in the hereafter and yet further from the road.[5]

It is the body of a man, therefore, through which he attains his goals. If the body becomes ill or weak, man is no longer able to benefit himself or those around him. So, Islam is the religion of the body and the soul. It provides a high standard of ethics and moral values for man to follow a straight path that results in harvesting the good of this world and that of the Hereafter.

Islam also denies total asceticism, for it may stunt life. Instead, it looks for the median that allows both body and soul to grow and develop. The Muslim is one whose inner self is absorbed in the love of his Lord, while his outer self faces the world fighting to correct it, and by doing this, perfects the belief in the Oneness of his Creator.

His love detaches his soul from all that is material, a love whose light purifies and strengthens not only the soul but the body that houses it, creating the perfect symbiosis energized and guided by the faith in the Most Compassionate God, Who says:

> And he who rejects false deities and believes in Allah has grasped a firm hand-hold which will never break. Allah is Hearer, Knower. Allah is the protecting friend of those who believe. He brings them out of darkness and into light.[6]

The fruits of such guidance are men who strive to purify themselves and look to create the perfect society whose foundation is piety. These men see the differences in races as a sign of the majesty of their Creator and, in so doing, strengthen the bond of faith that lies between them.

---

[5]T.Q., Sura 17, Isra, verse 72.
[6]T.Q., Sura 2, The Cow, verses 256-257.

O humankind! We created you from a single pair of a male and
female, and made you into nations and tribes, that ye may know
each other (not that ye may despise each other). Verily the
most honored of you in the sight of Allah is the most righteous
of you, Allah is Knower, Aware.[7]

Thus, the compassion of Islam lies in its seeing mankind as one
brotherhood. For the prophet of God said: **"All creation is the
dependent of Allah and the most beloved of His creation is the
most beneficent to those under his care."** An example of such care
and concern is seen in the life of the prophet who, when a funeral bier
of a Jew passed by him, stood up out of respect. When asked about his
action he replied: **"Is it not a soul?"** It is by such demonstrations of
sincerity and love for mankind that the Qur `ān —the word of Allah
(God)—gives testimony to the mission of its prophet as a mission of
mercy to all.

And We did not send you save as a mercy to all of creation.[8]

The Qur `ān further describes the call of its prophet as an address
to the intellect of mankind towards a willing acceptance of humility
based on conviction rather than forced submission.

Let there be no compulsion in religion. Truth stands out clear
from Error.[9]

The very word 'Islam' means the willing submission of creation to
its Lord. The prophet said: **"Lo the friends of Allah are those when
seen remind others of Him."**[10] For the believer is as the sun during a
beautiful sunset or the full moon on a clear night. They are signs of the
wonders of this universe that remind one of the beauty of the Creator.
"Allah is beautiful and loves all that is beautiful."[11] It is a beauty that
stems from the conformity of such bodies to the plan and design of their
Creator. Thus, when a believer reaches a state where his submission is

---

[7] T.Q., Sura 49, verse 13.
[8] T.Q., Sura 21, The Prophets, verse 107.
[9] T.Q., Sura 2, The Cow, verse 256.
[10] Narrated by Al-Hakem in Al-Jame Al-Sageer, Vol. 1, p. 111.
[11] Narrated by Muslim, Chapter of Al-Kibir, "The Arrogance."

complete, it is at that stage that he parallels the universe surrounding him and is as his intended design.

Surely We did create man in the best of molds.[12]

The prophet of God said: **"The heirs of the prophets are the scholars."**[13] However, the prophets of God do not leave behind scholarly works as such, but bequeathed an infinitely more important legacy to man: knowledge and wisdom acquired from their Creator. The prophets came to teach and purify man under the instructions and direction of His Lord.

The legacy of Islam is seen in the sincere people who dedicate themselves to the betterment of humanity and improving the welfare of mankind. It is around such persons that men have gathered and will continue to gather to learn of their religion and their Creator.

In it are men who love to be purified and Allah loves those who look to purify themselves.[14]

A DIVINE MISSION

The mission of all God's apostles and prophets (peace be upon them) was based on an essential corner stone and well grounded pillar; that is, to guide human beings to the existence of the Creator of the universe. Therefore, mankind must believe in, and worship God in order to be happy and lead a righteous life. Besides, God's apostles emphasized the fraternity of human creatures who God created (Adam and Eve were their parents); the criteria of excellence being piety, righteousness and virtuous deeds.[15]

As a result of belief in God and the fraternity of all human beings, mankind must necessarily live a life of love, agreement, cooperation and peace. All of God's legislation was revealed to emphasize this purpose. The prophets of God at various times showed humanity that God's religion is always the same. They are intimate brothers with no enmity

---

[12]T.Q., Sura 95, verse 4.
[13]Narrated by Abu Dawood, Al-Termethy and Ibn Majah, Chapter of The Knowledge
[14]T.Q., Sura 9, Repentance, verse 108.
[15]See Page 8, T.Q., Sura 49, verse 13.

or conflict, that the aim of their message is one, that He who raised them is One, and that the fundamentals of their religions are one—void of any contradiction or contrast. The Qur`ān says:

> He has ordained for you that religion which he commanded unto Noah, and that which We inspire in you, and that which We commanded unto Abraham and Moses and Jesus, saying: "Establish (the religion) and be not divided therein."[16]

This text testifies to the premise that God's religion at all times and with all prophets is undoubtedly the same, and that God orders His prophets and their people to unite and agree and not to be different and separate. The following verse is one of many which confirms this.

> We have sent thee Inspiration, as We sent it to Noah and the Messengers after him: We sent Inspiration to Abraham, Ishmael, Isaac, Jacob and the Tribes, to Jesus, Job, Jonah, Aaron and Solomon, and to David We gave the Psalms.[17]

God' revelation is consistent in quality and topic. Thus, all prophets draw from one main spring or source. Moreover, it is evident that the Qur`ān orders the Muslims to believe in all God's prophets and to obey their commandments:

> Say (O Muslims): 'we believe in God and that which is revealed unto us and that which was revealed unto Abraham, and Ishmael, and Isaac, and Jacob and the Tribes, and that which Moses and Jesus received and that which the Prophets received from their Lord. We make no distinction between any of them: And we bow to God (in Islam).[18]

Several long Suras (chapters) throughout the Qur`ān ennoble and dignify Christ and his mother, Virgin Mary. The Qur`ān also mentions and clarifies Christ's miracles and it tells of miracles not found in the Gospel itself, such as creating birds out of clay into which he breathed life with God's permission. Another miracle of Jesus is speaking to people from the cradle.

---

[16]T.Q., Sura 42, The Counsel, verse 13.
[17]T.Q., Sura 4, The Women, verse 163.
[18]T.Q., Sura 2, The Cow, verse 136.

In the Qur`ān, there are two long Suras specifically pertaining to Christ: the first is Mary and the second is The Imran Family, the family of Jesus Christ. In these two Suras, we are told of Mary's giving birth to Christ after receiving the news of her conception through the Holy Spirit Gabriel:

> And when the angels said: O Mary! Behold, God has chosen you and made you pure, and has preferred you above (all) the women of creation... O Mary! Behold, God gives you glad tidings of a word from Him, whose name is Messiah, Jesus, son of Mary, illustrious in the world and the Hereafter, and one of those brought near to God. He will speak unto mankind in his cradle and in his manhood, and he is of the righteous.[19]

The Qur`ān addresses the Muslims clearly indicating Christ's high rank with God:

> The Messiah, Jesus, son of Mary, was a messenger of God and His word which He conveyed unto Mary, and a spirit from Him.[20]

These ideas, or more precisely, this belief which Muslims are ordered to embrace about Christ and Christianity made their hearts open to receive all of Christ's teachings and facilitated convergence and cooperation between Muslims and Christians, under the good care of the Qur`ān and the Apostle of Islam and all the believers. The Qur`ān shows, very clearly, the Christians are the closest to Muslims on account of the good morals and virtues they share with them. It says:

> And you will find the nearest of them in affection to those who believe are those who say: 'Lo! We are Christians. That is because there are among them priests and monks, and because they are not given to arrogance. When they listen to that which has been revealed unto the messenger, you see their eyes overflow with tears because of their recognition of the truth. They say: 'Our Lord, we believe.' 'Inscribe us as among the witnesses'... God has rewarded them for their saying Gardens

---

[19]T.Q., Sura 4, The Family of Imran, verses 42-46.
[20]T.Q., Sura 4, The Women, verse 171.

underneath which rivers flow, wherein they abide forever. That is the reward of the good.[21]

As a result of this positive attitude of Islam towards Christianity and the Gospel, many ancient Christians were moved to express their belief and recognition of Mohammad and his religion. Some of them even granted the Muslims moral and financial aid to solidify and propagate Islam, such as the Emperor of Ethiopia (Abyssinia) in the 6th century C.E., who asked the oppressed Muslims who migrated to this country to recite some verses from the Qur `ān concerning Christ and his faith. The Emperor, as well as his monks, wept and declared their recognition of Mohammad's prophethood. He said: the teachings of Christ and Mohammad flow out from one source. That Emperor did not give up Christianity when he said that, for Islam does not expect Christians to ignore the commandments and teachings of Jesus Christ. The Qur `ān addresses Christians:

Let the people of the Gospel judge by that which God has revealed therein.[22]

And:

We bestowed on him (Jesus) the Gospel wherein is guidance and light.[23]

Prophet Mohammad said: **"I am the closest of all people to Jesus, son of Mary"**. He also said: **"We prophets are brethren, our father is one, and our mothers are different, but with one religion"**.[24] The companions of the prophet and the great leaders of Islam used to say to their contemporary Christians: **"We do not prevent you from believing in Christianity; indeed, we order you to obey it"**.[25] Such examples are countless.

---

[21]T.Q., Sura 5, The Flood, verses 82-85.

[22]T.Q., Sura 5, The Flood, verse 47.

[23]T.Q., Sura 5, the Flood, verse 46.

[24]Narrated by Mulim as well as by Al-Bukhari, Vol. 1, Pg. 255, Chapter of Prophets are Brothers

[25]Hateb Ibn Abi Balta'a addressing Al Mukaukes, The King of Egypt. Narrated by Ibn Sa'ad in Al-Tabakat Al-Kubra, Vol. 1, Pg. 260

HISTORICAL EXAMPLES OF ISLAMIC BEHAVOIR
TOWARD CHRISTIANS

To show the utmost degree of fraternity, love, affection and collaboration, Prophet Moḥammad made his mosque a place for worship for the Christian delegations in Medina when they came to inquire about Islam.

In Syria, although this is no longer practiced, the Muslims made of their great Omayyad Mosque, a joint temple of worship for Muslims and Christians. Everyone entered it through one gate, when Damascus was the capital of their great state. They divided the mosque into two parts and they used to worship simultaneously.

In Jerusalem, Omar Ibn Al-Khattab, the second Caliph, refused to say his Salah (prayers) in the Holy Sepulcher lest the Muslims turn that church, or part of it, into a Mosque. Thus, he prayed next to it and observed its sanctity. All this was the inevitable outcome of understanding the great propinquity and respect between these two great revealed religions in ancient times.

Prophet Moḥammad commanded Muslims to be kind to Jews and Christians, the followers of the two revealed religions. He said: "Whoever causes mischief to a Christian or a Jew shall be my enemy on doomsday and he shall pay for it."[26] He also said: "You Muslims shall conquer Egypt. If so, be kind to its Coptic Christian people."[27]

In Egypt, when the son of the Muslim governor of Egypt beat a Christian on his head after a quarrel, the latter went to Omar, the Caliph in Medina, asking for justice. Omar summoned the governor and his son and gave the Christian a whip to beat his opponent in the presence of the great men of the state. After the Christian took his revenge, he abstained from beating the governor himself when Omar asked him to, saying: "I have received justice. Christians pray to God to reward You!" Turning to his governor, Omar said: "Why do you enslave the freely born people?"

Islam has not stopped at this border concerning affection for other revealed religions. It has gone further and implanted love, shown by genuine emotions and feelings. When the Persian idolaters defeated the

---

[26]Narrated by Al-Tabarani Fil Awsat
[27]Narrated by Al-Hakem, Vol. 1, Pg. 553. "Life of the Prophet" events of the 7th year of Hijra, Chapter of Sending Ambassadors to the Kings

Byzantine Christians, Prophet Mohammad and the Muslims, at that time, were suffering the persecution of the pagans in Mecca. When they got the news they grieved. Gabriel descended, consoled the Muslims and brought good tidings that the Christians would be victorious in less than nine years. This event occurs in the Sura which was titled Al Roum, the "Roman Byzantine".

> Alif. Lam. Mim. Defeated have been the Byzantines in the lands close-by; yet it is they who, notwithstanding their defeat, shall be victorious within a few years: with God rests all power of decision, first and last. And on that day will the believers rejoice in God's succor: He gives succor to whomever He wills, since He alone is Almighty, the Dispenser of grace.[28]

The prophecy came true and the Muslims were delighted. Islam, by its teachings and principles, has been able to turn millions of infidels into believers in God, in Christ, in Mohammad, and in all prophets and revealed testaments.

THE ONENESS OF GOD

The same theological doctrine about God, the Creator, the Matchless, the Partnerless Lord, is clearly illustrated in the Bible and in the Qur`ān. In St. John's Gospel, Christ says: **"And this is life eternal, that they might know thee, the only true God, and Jesus Christ whom thou hast sent."** In St. Mathew we read: **"....to the Lord, your God, kneel, and Him alone worship."** God addresses Mohammad in the Qur`ān saying:

"Say: He is God, the One!" and:

"Know there is no god but God."

When Christ was asked about doomsday, he said: **"None knows when that day and that hour comes."** The same was told to Mohammad in the Holy Qur`ān:

---

[28].T.Q., Sura 30, The Romans, verses 1-5.

They ask thee of the (destined) Hour, when it will come to port. Say: 'Knowledge thereof is with my Lord only. He will alone manifest it at its proper time.'[29]

There are countless texts in the Qur`ān and the Bible which suggests that the two religions agree on the worship of the Almighty, Sole-Creator. Thus, it is taken for granted that there should be trifling differences in interpretation, which occur even among followers of one religion. Thereof, this ought not to prevent compromise and accord of hearts and spiritual affiliation for the benefit of peace, faith and mankind, the likeness of which is a bouquet of variegated flowers that dazzles and fascinates when arranged in good proportion.

Abraham established the original foundation of this building by combating idolatry and thus raising the standard of monotheism. This standard was upheld and heralded by his successors, Moses, Jesus, and Moḥammad, the latter to whom the Seal of Prophet was given. Moḥammad refers to this analogy of a building in the following tradition:

"I and the previous prophets are exemplified in a mansion built and beautified by someone save a space left in a corner for a missing block. People entered and admiringly exhorted him, 'Do lay this block', I have been this block and I am the final and ultimate prophet."

This tradition of prophethood outlines the gradual process by which God has perfected His religion. Moḥammad's mission, therefore, is deeply rooted in the origins of the former religions.

Every religion that has been decreed by God holds a faith or belief in God that is absolute and pertains to the affairs of both this world and the next. The preaching of the prophets, as ordained by God, was not restricted to those people who lived around them, it encompassed more comprehensive and vaster horizons. Jesus and Moḥammad, for example, were sent to illuminate the souls of the whole of humanity, and not just to the people of Jerusalem or Mecca.

Jesus said: **"I have come as a savoir to the world;"** and God states in the Qur`ān outlining the prophetic mission of Moḥammad:

---

[29]T.Q., Sura 7, The Heights, verse 187.

And We did not send you except as a mercy to all of mankind.[30]

We can see the results and the reality of both their universal missions, as Islam and Christianity are the largest of the world's religions. Also today, with the advances in technology and the increase in luxury, ease, and leisure these advances facilitate, religious values are diminished. This is coupled with an increase in anxiety levels, as the ever-growing materialistic civilization increases in its material acquisitiveness, greed, and a lack of God-consciousness. It is because of this that man finds himself in a constant state of moral confusion, bewildered and let down by the false promises of his technological world.

The resulting numbness in consciousness that has developed today has led man to ignore religion and the spiritual values it holds, unwilling to allow his heart to fill with hope. Hope is a concept that has become altogether unfamiliar to today's generation that has seen little but shattered dreams: Once bitten twice shy! Furthermore, these shattered dreams have resulted in a vacuum that neither entertainment clubs, dance halls, nor pleasures of the flesh can fill. These escapes from the realities of the world represent nothing more than a desperate attempt to relieve pent-up frustrations in destructive ways. They are purposeless and aimless. This seeking of fleeting pleasures and material idolatry lowers man to the level of a beast, making him harmful and irresponsible to himself and all that is around him.

Material good or technology must be man's servant not his master. He must keep his pleasures under control, rather than being controlled by them. The essentials and fundamentals of religion are not responsible for this degradation, but the inability of the clergy to lead men to faith and conviction.

Divine religion is essentially guidance for all who are lost, a source of goodness for all, and a path of righteousness for those who struggle to live in dignity and happiness. In short, it is the perfect idea to pursue.

But personal interpretations, superficial reflections on texts, or worn out literal translations have darkened true religion which in the past, used to illuminate man's path with love and peace.

Religion has never failed to enhance man's spiritual or material needs. The divine doctrine granted by Christianity and Islam endows

---

[30]T.Q., Sura 21, The Prophets, verse 107.

mankind with the ability to withstand excessive pleasures and desires. Thus, religious conviction frees man to pursue maximum productivity in all fields in which he engages.

RESPONSIBILITY OF RELIGIOUS PERSONS

The mission of those who believe in God and His apostles, is to stress this fact by practice, by carrying the torch to guide those who have erred in order to rescue humanity from the stagnant filth it lies in. We must not profess disability but must reconsider our methods of dealing with people, acknowledging our faults in order to correct them.

On the whole those, who abandon religion, do so not out of animosity towards God, the Creator, but rather most probably because they found their clergyman to be a fanatic, or an extreme puritan, backward in this thinking that clashed with sound reasoning and the scientific approach. Consequently, what is required from clergymen today is valor, wisdom, and sincerity, particularly towards those lacking in morals and faith, who have rejected religion as if it were an underdone dish. We must prepare our food for the soul and mind to be delicious for all. Our job must consist in elevating man's humanity and our role must be like physicians who dispense medicine with tenderness and sympathy. We must not condemn our fellow men as atheists, for this judgment is God's alone, as man's actions are determined by his sincerity which only God sees. Repentance erases past sins as God's mercy encompasses all the sins of the world.

Jesus Christ said: **Heaven's delight in the repentance of one sinner exceeds its joyfulness at securing ninety-nine faithful people who do not need to repent.** Mohammad said: **God extends His forgiveness by night so that those who have wronged themselves by day might repent, as He also extends it during the day so that those who have wronged themselves by night might find repentance.**[31] Jesus said: **I have not come to destroy nay but to serve,** and he also said: **I want mercy and not a sacrifice.**

As religious persons, we should take into consideration the changes in contemporary man's nature. In the past, people readily accepted the lessons clergymen taught without argument. Today, we find modern

---

[31]Narrated by Muslim and Al-Nassai, Chapter of Repentance.

man free from such mental servitude. He criticizes everything freely and in particular religions, including their doctrines, dogmas and adherents. Men of today do not accept anything that fails to satisfy their intellect and scientific bent. Therefore, as men of religion, we should do away with unreasonable and faulty practices that have distorted the essence and brilliance of true religion in the eyes of our contemporaries.

To do this, how should religion in this century be presented? Mohammad and Christ both preached faith by common sense, dialogue, and ethical conduct. A deep conviction in his beliefs, seen in his actions and his relationship with god, led Christ to acknowledge Mohammad, whose advent was yet to come. In the Qur`ān, God speaks of this:

> And (tell) of Jesus, who said to the Israelites: 'I am sent forth to you by Allah to confirm the Torah already revealed and to give news of an apostle that will come after me whose name is Ahmad'. (Ahmad is another name of Mohammad's, meaning 'Praised One').[32]

The clergy today, in particular, hardly have any of the above-mentioned characteristics. In the past, things were easier and faith was propagated despite the poor standard of education because their contemporaries were simple-hearted men who could be converted easily. At the time idols were made of wood or stone, so they were easily conquered. Now the state of affairs is more complex: idols are fleshy desires, ideologies and international doctrines, all of which had at their disposal the modern media creating intensive propaganda campaigns on their behalf that few can resist. The separation, therefore, between religion and modern man has deepened; faith and love have decreased and dwindled, while egocentricity and lewdness have become more predominant and are on the rise.

If humanity does not receive deliverance through the people of profound integrity and faith working in acquaintance and religious toleration, the situation will be awful and God will rebuke us in the world. Hereafter for every shortcoming, fanaticism and discord that may promote devastation, agony and bloodshed.

---

[32]T.Q., Sura 61, Battle Array, verse 6.

Remedies are available; the illness is pernicious and it calls for operations by physicians of the heart and soul who have excellent prescriptions to rid humanity of wretchedness and ruin.

Considering the resolutions that the world religious conference has made — the Vatican declared in the clearest terms that Islam is a revealed religion. This is a step forward. The conference in Cordova, in 1977, declared that Moḥammad *is **the prophet and apostle of God**.*[33] These and many others make us hopeful that the future will be replete with goodness, cooperation and love between the revealed religions, as they are branches from the tree of Abraham. When this goal is achieved, humility will lead an affectionate and peaceful life that will exclude ruin and devastation.

We have come to know Christ and Christians through our Qurʾān and the teachings of our Prophet; therefore, know us. We shook hands with you, embraced you, studied you and we respect Christ and his revealed Gospel and his Virgin Mother; therefore, shake hands with us, embrace us, study us and reciprocate in the same terms or better.

Our being remote from each other resembles two brothers who have been lost for several years. One day, one of them wandering in a wasteland catches sight of some distant object which he takes for a beast. He is proceeding to kill it when, on approaching closer and closer, he meets his long lost brother fact to face. They embrace and shed tears of joy at reunion after such a long absence.

We are in need of coming nearer and nearer until we embrace and meet in full understanding. This will soon be effected by the cooperative efforts of all sincere and faithful adherents of every religion. God will assist us as long as we support His cause. God will give victory to those who make His cause victorious. May the peace and God's mercy and blessings be on all of us.

---

[33]The 2nd International Conference held in Spain by "the Islamic Christian Friendship Committee," March 21-27, 1977, attended by 200 researchers from Egypt, Tunisia, Syria and other countries. *Al-Arabi Magazine*, Issue # 223, June 1977, Pg. 40.

Islam and Franciscanism

Prophet Moḥammad of Arabia and St. Francis of Assisi in the Spirituality of Mission

Fareed Munir Ph.D.

Introduction

Today, Islam and Christianity are the two largest religions in the world; eighteen percent of the world's population are Muslims and thirty three percent are Christians, together making up about half of the global population.[1] They show the greatest growth among all religions. Although western Asia is the birthplace of both traditions, the largest concentrations of both religions are far removed from that area. Indonesia has the largest Muslim population and the United States has the largest Christian population. Both religions include different groups, but each has one dominant—for Muslims eighty three percent are Sunnis (followers of the traditions of Moḥammad and for Christians fifty seven percent are Roman Catholics.

This reveals three points that are at the heart of this study: one, it is from an Islamic perspective. Obviously, Islam and Franciscanism are two separate traditions, but it is not my intent to overplay the differences.[2] But, my intent is to recognize the distinctness of mission within both traditions, particularly the Islamic religion. Thus, I will use the Islamic religion as an interpretive tool and lens to better understand the Franciscan tradition which will allow me also the ability to create an ideological dialogue about the notion of mission between Sultan al-Kamil and St. Francis. Additionally, my discussion about Sultan al-Kamil—a devout follower of Prophet Moḥammad—and St. Francis will allow me to be able to connect the lives of both Prophet Moḥammad and St. Francis who were not contemporaries of one another. This

---

[1]William E. Phipps, *Muhammad and Jesus: A Comparison of the Prophets and Their Teachings* (New York: Continuum Publishing Company, 1996), 11, 249.

[2]John Corrigan, Frederick M. Denny, Carlos M.N. Eire, and Martin S. Jaffee, *Jews, Christians, Muslims: A Comparative Introduction to Monotheistic Religions* (New Jersey: Prentice Hall, 1998), xi.

study then focuses on the general ideology shared by the majority of Muslims within the Sunni line of thought. As for the Christian perspective, this study looks at general ideological notions within Christianity, but specifically the Franciscan tradition within Roman Catholicism; two, both Islam and Christianity possess a sense of universal message or spirituality and, three, both religions developed a strong missionary emphasis from their beginnings.[3]

Prophet Moḥammad and St. Francis

The central stories of both Islam and Franciscanism center around a major person, Prophet Moḥammad of Arabia (570-632 ce) for Islam and St. Francis of Assisi (1182-1226 ce) for Franciscanism. Both men are held in the highest regard by millions of people and followers. Each man is considered by his respective tradition a model of conduct for spirituality and mission.[4] They are both exemplars of their respective positions on the notion of mission. Thus, through Prophet Moḥammad one can mature spiritually and become a true Muslim and missionary and, as well, it is through St. Francis that one can mature and become a true Christian and missionary.

Hence, much of the uniqueness of Islam and Franciscanism is based on the character of these founders.[5] Although Prophet Moḥammad and St. Francis were not contemporaries, both of them in their respective periods possessed the deepest regard for God, and both possessed a belief in humanity's propensity to worship that God. Therefore, Prophet Moḥammad's and St. Francis's belief and practice of both these major principles act to symbolically unite them. For purposes of my study then it is appropriate to reconstruct both men's views on the idea of mission.

According to the Islamic tradition, God through the Arch-Angel Jibreel began the revelation of the Qur 'ān to Prophet Moḥammad in

---

[3]Phipps, 11, also see John L. Esposito, *The Islamic Threat: Myth or Reality?* (New York: Oxford University Press, 1992), 25; and see Frederick Mathewson Denny, *An Introduction to Islam* 2nd ed. (New York: Macmillan Publishing Company, 1994), 40.

[4]The Editorial Board, *Build With the Living Stones: a Program of Study on the Franciscan Missionary Charism* Revised Edition (Silver Spring, Maryland: The Franciscan Mission Service, 1989), 9/1.

[5]Phipps, 12.

610 ce. Prior to the revelation the Prophet was a contemplative person. He would withdraw from the world by going to a cave, called <u>Hira</u>. He used this time to contemplate the world that surrounded him. His search to discover the truth was rooted in the realities of the physical world. The Prophet's contemplative search, ultimately, cleansed him spiritually of the secular ideology of his day, making him no longer a dependent on the status quo beliefs held by the majority.[6] The Qur 'ān [Muslim Holy Book] states,

By time

Verily Man is lost [if he does not use time wisely]. . . . (ciii, 1-2)

Prophet Mohammad was a man that used time wisely; he withdrew and contemplated the notion of God and the physical world because he desired to be connected with God's way. In essence, he chose to achieve the best of what God offered humanity. His contemplation and complete faith in God empowered him mentally and spiritually to return to the very world that he had left in order to carry out actions that benefited humanity.

These points stated above about the Prophet Mohammad may be brought to bear also on the character of St. Francis. He "wanted to be nothing else but a man of contemplation."[7] And for him Christian contemplation inherently contained faith and good deeds, that is actions of service to humanity. Thus St. Francis believed that there should be no separation between the Franciscan Order, complete faith in God, and humanity.[8] Concomitantly, the world was God's challenge to the believer; it represented a place where one could develop mentally and spiritually in God's way, despite the false ideologies, wars, and violence of his day.[9]

---

[6] Muhammad Husayn Haykal, *The Life of Muhammad* 8th ed. (United States: North American Trust Publications, 1976), 71-73.

[7] The Editorial Board, 10/1.

[8] Editorial Board, 10/1.

[9] Hoeberichts, 66.

Islam and Mission

There are approximately one billion Muslims that span the globe today. Muslims continue to spread their message successfully throughout Europe, Asia, Africa, and North America. There are more than forty-four Muslim countries that extend from Senegal to Indonesia, and significant Muslim populations may be found in such diverse places as the former Soviet Union, China, India, England, and the United States. Islam is the second, only to Christianity, largest religion, making it a world presence.[10]

The spread of Islam over such a vast portion of the globe is due to various causes, social, political, and religious; but among these one of the most powerful factors at work in the production of this remarkable result has been the unrelenting efforts of Muslim missionaries, who envisioned and affirmed the Prophet as their model. The duty of propagation of the religion, called dawa in Arabic, is not an after-thought in the history of Islam; all believers are enjoined from the beginning.[11]

The Holy Scripture of Muslims is called al-Qur 'ān [the recitation]. It is the Book of God and it contains 114 sura/s [chapters] and over 6,000 aya/s [verses]. There are two types of chapters. One type consisting of ninety suras is the Meccan or early chapters that were revealed to the Prophet by the Arch-Angel Jibreel [Gabriel] in Mecca (modern day Saudi Arabia) the first twelve years of his prophethood. The other type is the Medinan suras consisting of twenty-four chapters that were revealed the last ten years of his mission in Medina (modern day Saudi Arabia). Hence the Qur 'ān was revealed to the Prophet over a twenty-three year span. Over that twenty-three year period, Prophet Moḥammad received revelation occasionally from God on the notion of mission, which acted to reinforce its importance. Two early Meccan verses gave credence to this; they state,

> Invite all to the way of your Lord with wisdom and beautiful preaching [Moḥammad]; and argue with them in ways that are

---

[10]John L. Esposito, *Islam: The Straight Path* 3rd ed. (New York: Oxford University Press, 1998), 1.

[11]T. W. Arnold, *The Preaching of Islam: A History of the Propagation of the Muslim Faith* (London: Constable & Company LTD, 1913), 3.

best and most gracious; for your Lord knows best, ..." (xvi, 125)

> . . .Call (or invite them to the faith), and stand steadfast as you are commanded, nor follow you their vain desires; but say, "I believe in the Book which God has sent down.... (xlii, 15)

And, later Medinan verses further state,

> . . . And say to the People of the Book (Jews and Christians) and to those who are unlearned [Moḥammad]: Do you (also) submit yourselves? If they do, they are in right guidance, but if they turn back, your duty is to convey the Message; and in God's sight are (all) His servants. (iii, 20)

And again,

> To every people have We appointed rites and ceremonies which they must follow; let them not then dispute with you on the matter, but do you invite (them) to your Lord [Moḥammad]; for you art assuredly on the right way. (xxii, 67-69).[12]

Therefore, Islam was a missionary religion both in theory and in practice from its inception. As well, the life of the Prophet stands as a model of missionary conduct.[13]

For this reason, modern Islamic scholars have argued that Islam is history's first global civilization. They asserted that between political and military conquest, but mainly missionary activity by traders, Sufi brotherhoods (mystics), itinerant preachers (men and women), and the

---

[12]Abdullah Yusuf Ali translator, *The Holy Qur 'an: Text, Translation and Commentary* (United States: McGregor & Werner, Inc., 1946).

All verses are quotes from the Abdullah Yusuf Ali translation of the Qur 'an. Where there are words in parenthesis within a verse, these are words that Abdullah Yusuf Ali has added for clarity of meaning. Technically, Muslims only accept the original Arabic Qur 'an, although there are many translations. It is important to note then that Abdullah Yusuf Ali has two types of translations of the Qur 'an; one, a translation of the Qur 'an from the Arabic to the English language only; and two, a translation from Arabic to English language with commentary on the verses of the Qur 'an. For this study, I will use the second type of text. Thus, it should be understood that the latter part of my study where Ali's commentary is used are his interpretations of certain verses, and not the Qur 'an.

[13]Arnold, 3-5.

common believers (lasting from the seventh century to the seventeenth century) that Muslims brought together a single overarching civilization. In addition, Muslims synthesized elements from civilizations of the Old World such as, Irano-Semitic, Malay-Javanese, and Greco-Roman, that contributed to their becoming global missionaries. They evolved a distinctive civilization that proved one of the most vital and durable the world has ever seen. In fact, the conversion of mass populations through the usage of the Qur 'ān and Sunnah (i.e., Prophets example) to Islam and the ability of Muslim culture to absorb, adapt, and retransmit Islamic socio-religious values allowed for the survival as well the flourishing of the Muslim world.[14]

Signs of Islamic History in the Abbasid Period

Prophet Moḥammad's death resulted in the <u>Rashidun Caliphs</u> (632-661), the four consecutive successors who led a centralized government from Medina. They were responsible for the maintenance and continuation of the religio-political mission established by the Prophet. Subsequently, the religio-political mission shifted outside of Arabia into the hands of two successive dynasties by the second half of the seventh century. The two dynasties were the Umayyad, which governed the Muslim <u>umma</u> [community] from Damascus, Syria between 661and 750 ce; and a counter dynasty the Abbasid, which led and ruled from its capital city of Baghdad, Iraq until 1258 ce.[15]

Concerning the Abbassid dynasty, history reflects that they attempted to prove their adherence to the original religio-political notion of mission more than their predecessors had done. Abbasid rule was no longer meant to be Arab, as it had been under the Umayyad, but rather it was meant to be Islamic, based on the religio-political mission and conduct of the Prophet Moḥammad.

More recent studies on the Abbasid period show that non-Muslims, for example Christians, found it easier to tolerate and even convert to Islam under the Abbassid rule because Islamic ideas and

---

[14]Richard M. Eaton, *Islamic History as Global History* (Washington: American Historical Association, 1990), 17.

[15]Eaton, 17-18.

attitudes revealed an affinity to Christianity. For example, the Muslims institutionalized charity like Christians; they shared praying and fasting like Christians, and many other features. Furthermore, these studies help to explicate and dispute earlier cruder Christian models and notions of mission during the Abbassid period which tended to conflate the idea of mission to non-Muslims into a single process, Islam as the religion of the sword.[16]

Such notions were developed in response to the important idea that within one hundred years Islam had expanded to Europe. Muslims regarded themselves as carriers of a global mission, and not just members of an Arab cult. Consequently, they found themselves with their new leadership roles ruling over a plurality of autonomous and self-regulating religious communities, including Christians. Choices about the religio-political nature of mission and its character as it relates to the Qur 'ān and Sunnah became much more complicated. For this reason, during the Abbasid period the notion of mission as it related to an independent Islamic identity amidst the older religious communities, as the Christian ones, obligated Muslims to bring all these diverse communities and traditions together into a new religio-political synthesis under the concept of mission. On that account, mission acted to transcend all of the religious communities, including the Islamic communities, which ultimately supplanted all other counter notions of religious propagation. The fact that Muslims consciously saw themselves as playing a unifying role in broadening the notion of mission to that of an integral whole by uniting separate religious and linguistic communities into a single religious identity, seems to be the tone of the Qur 'ān's verses exhorting Christians to leave aside their differences and return to the pure, unadulterated monotheism of Abraham, their common ancestor.[17] The Qur 'ān states,

> Say: Oh People of the Book (Jews and Christians)! Come to common terms as between us and you; that we worship none but God; that we associate no partners with Him; that we erect not, from among ourselves Lords and patrons other than God. . .(iii, 64)

---

[16]Eaton, 20.
[17]Eaton, 20-22.

As an invitation intended for the "People of the Book" Christians (and Jews), these words of the Qur 'ān point to the unifying role of mission in the process of Muslim's gradual development of their religio-political worldview in the Abbassid period.

This is not to suggest that all members of the Muslim communities and rulers, although theoretically equal in status under the Qur 'ān, perfectly implemented and followed this ideal of mission throughout the Abbasid period; but, by the time of the Sultan (i.e., honorific title—leader) al-Kamil Moḥammad (.d 1238) of the Ayyubid family (i.e., dynasty 1193-1249) this ideal was highly regarded.

On his death (d. 1193), the great Salah al-Adin Ibn Ayyub (Saladin) left his power to his sons and brothers as the leaders of chief states.[18] Sultan al-Kamil the nephew of Saladin was the leader of Egypt. Although little is known of the Sultan's personal understanding of mission, history has left him favorably as a member and ruler of the Abbasid period. He has been characterized as an honorable, fair, and just Muslim. Hence, in accepting the Sultan's character and for the purpose of my study, certain theoretical presumptions can be made by linking him with the description and practice of mission in the Abbasid period. In other words, he was a sincere Muslim who practiced the Sunnah or conduct of the Prophet.

The Legacy of the Crusades

Sultan al-Kamil was a leader during the period of the Crusades, which take their name from the "cross" (*crux* in Latin). They were a series of eight military expeditions extending from the eleventh to the thirteenth centuries which pitted Christendom (the Christian armies of the Franks) against Islam (the Muslim armies of the Saracens).[19] Although it is not the purpose of this study to revisit the Crusades, it is important to mention certain points about the Crusades from an Islamic perspective, which will further contribute to the development of the Sultan's notion of mission. His notion of mission, particularly around the time of the fifth Crusade, will play an important role in

---

[18]Marshall G. D. Hodgson, *The Venture of Islam: Conscience and History in a World Civilization* 2nd vol. (Chicago: The University of Chicago Press, 1974), 267.

[19]Esposito, *The Islamic Threat* 40.

understanding the relationship that was established during St. Francis's visit with the Sultan al-Kamil in 1219 ce.

In the modern period, two myths pervade Western perceptions of the Crusades: first, Christendom triumphed; and second, the Crusades were fought for the liberation of the Holy areas (e.g., Jerusalem). But, the specific facts of the Crusades are little known. For Christians, the Crusades took on an extraordinary place in history; and for Muslims, the memory of the Crusades, at best, lived on as the clearest example of militant Christianity, a reminder of Christianity's earliest hostility toward Islam. Therefore, for Muslim-Christian relations historically, it is less a case of what actually happened in the Crusades than how they are remembered by both communities. According to one Islamic scholar, Esposito;

> Jerusalem was a city sacred to all three Abrahamic faiths. . . . Under Muslim rule, Christian churches and populations were left unmolested. Christian shrines and relics had become popular pilgrimage sites for Christendom. Jews, long banned from living there by Christian rulers, were permitted to return, live, and worship in the city of Solomon and David. Muslims built a shrine, the Dome of the Rock, and a mosque, the al-Aqsa, near the Wailing Wall, the last remnant of Solomon's Temple, and thus a site especially significant to Judaism. Five centuries of peaceful coexistence were now shattered by a series of holy wars which pitted Christianity against Islam and left an enduring legacy of distrust and misunderstanding.[20]

With an already established precedent of holy war, the call to war by Popes, started by Urban II, and other religious leadership of Christendom, the Crusades continued for centuries. Thus the legacy of the Crusades ultimately depended on whether Christians or Muslims were telling the story.[21]

Having stated that, it is important to note that the theater of the Crusades was unmistakably Syria and Palestine: "it was there that most expeditions landed, that all the Frankish states were established, and

---

[20]Esposito, *The Islamic Threat* 40-41.
[21]Esposito, 40-42

nearly all the stages of war took place."[22] Though that be the case, in the minds of Muslim historians Egypt and its rulers played a pivotal role in the Crusades, though attacked less frequently than Syria, and particularly during the years 1218-21. Such lull periods allowed for the Muslims, for our purposes Sultan al-Kamil, to strive often for a non-military solution to the Crusader question.[23] As a Muslim, the Sultan was obligated to search for a non-military solution because the Qur'ān commands Muslims to accept peace over war.[24] It also commands a Muslim to seek peace even in the midst of war. The Qur'ān states,

> . . . do thou incline towards peace, and trust in God: for He is the One that heareth and knoweth (all things).

> Should they (enemies) intend to deceive thee,—verily God sufficeth thee: He it is that hath strengthened thee with his aid and with (the company of) the believers;

> And (moreover) He hath put affection between their (the believers) hearts; not if thou hadst spent all that is in the earth couldst thou have produced that affection, but God Hath done it: for He is exalted in might, Wise. (viii, 61-62)

So, we can state then that in the Sultan's attempt to follow the example of the Prophet's sunnah [example], his aim was to establish a mission of peaceful coexistence with Christians. His sensitivity to the plight of Christians resulted in him making certain territorial concessions for them. Moreover, he was a man that demonstrated that he was more concerned with peace than war.[25] The Sultan was occupied with the idea of peace so much so that he has been captured in Islamic history as the Muslim who opposed those Muslims who were in favor of the Fifth Crusade. Instead, he preferred a pact with Frederick II, a Christian representative.[26] Such was the milieu and man

---

[22]Emmanuel Sivan, *Interpretations of Islam: Past and Present* (Princeton: The Darwin Press, 1985), 23.

[23]Sivan, 24-26.

[24]Maulana Muhammad Ali, *The Religion of Islam: A Comprehensive Discussion of the Sources, Principles and the Practices of Islam* 3rd ed. (Lahore: Ripon Printing Press, 1971), 460-61.

[25]Sivan, 27-28; according to Sivan, "One can barely find a mention [by Christian scholars] of the fact that it was really al-Kamil who invited Frederick to the Levant as an ally in the struggle against his brothers, the sultans of Syria and Mesopotamia."

[26]Sivan, 28.

al-Kamil that St. Francis of Assisi was allowed to visit for the purpose of Christian mission in 1219 ce.

St. Francis's Mission to the Muslims (Saracens)

If one among the rejecters [Christians] ask you for asylum, grant it to him, so that he may hear the Word of God; and then escort him where he can be secure.... (ix, 6)

In the modern period, it is fair to state that there is considerable confusion surrounding the term mission in Christianity.[27] Mission oftentimes implies missionary societies, paid agents, subscriptions, reports and journals, a missionary enterprise with a regularly constituted and continuous organization. On the contrary though, the word mission did not appear until the seventeenth century. Therefore, it did not mean initially the task of extending Christianity beyond the geographical limits and boundaries of what was then considered "Christian Europe."[28] For that reason, mission was carried out by all of God's believers, and particularly by special missionaries who in most cases were ordained priests or monks, missionary societies, and monastic orders.[29]

In other words, the earlier Church had a more integrated and holistic notion of mission; its idea of *propagatio fidei* was inclusive and all-embracing rather than restrictive. As one author put it, the Church was understood as "a community of believers that tries to articulate for itself first and then attempts to somehow disclose to the world the deep reasons for its profound and joyous hope. . . . [more clearly stated]: To evangelize [missionize] is like one beggar telling another one where he or she has found food."[30]

In the early history of the Church, then, the believers' primary responsibility of mission was peacefully to inform all people, including Muslims, that Christians had found food for one's mental and spiritual

---

[27]Richard G. Cote, O.M.I., *Re-visioning Mission: The Catholic Church and Culture in Postmodern America* (New York: Paulist Press, 1996), 6.

[28]Cote, 7-8.

[29]Arnold, 408.

[30]Cote, 7-8.

life. This raises two questions for my study: one, what happened to the Church's original notion of mission during the thirteenth century, the time of St. Francis? That notion when placed in its proper context, is similar to that of the Islamic religion's concept of mission; and two, why in St. Francis's time was it that his attitude and praxis of mission, which resembled that of the early Church, was out of touch with his time?

In the case of the first question, what happened? Christian sources suggest that during the time of St. Francis there had been formulated extreme views on mission that were shrouded in the ideology of the Crusades. For example, Muslims were presented for the most part as enemies of Christianity, and not as people in need of Christian mission; Christians had the view that Muslims were heretics, which made Muslims closer than pagans to Christians and less in need of Christian missionizing; there were those also who believed that there was a Islamic prohibition against Christians inviting Muslims to Christianity; and lastly, although a host of other reasons could be cited, there were some Christians who carried with them a tacit understanding that the Christian duty to spread the word to all people did not apply to Muslims.[31] Although most of these concepts were not based in reality, having no foundation whatsoever, they were inherently part of the Crusade ideology. As a result, they were transmitted from one generation to another through the channels of canon law and theology.[32]

The second question is: why in St. Francis's time did his attitude and praxis of mission, which resembled the early Church, was seemingly different from that of his time? In order to answer this question it is important to understand that this study has led me genuinely to the position that St. Francis's notion of mission was distinct. He was the first among the founders of a Religious Order to include in his mission called "the Rule" a special chapter on mission to

---

[31]Benjamin Z. Kedar, *Crusade and Mission: European Approaches toward the Muslims* (Princeton: Princeton University Press, 1984), 6-12; according to Kedar, these reasons on how Christians should or should not missionize Muslims have no foundation and are merely conjecture. He believes that probably Christians developed these ideas in response to the Muslim's resistance to convert to Christianity. Kedar believes that ultimately the Muslim's refusal to convert to Christianity became the rational or justification for waging war against them.

[32]Kedar, 202-03.

the Muslims (Saracens).[33] The career of St. Francis of Assisi is well known and it is not necessary to retell his story here. But it is important to state that St. Francis's notion of mission was based on the original teachings of the Church. For this reason, a case can be made that the inter-religious meeting between St. Francis and the Sultan al-Kamil was a successful one, despite the Crusade ideology and milieu that surrounded their coming together.

St. Francis viewed his mission and that of his Friars as universal in nature. In his early Rule, called the *Regula non Bullata* written in 1221, he seeks to call all people and all nations to the way of God. Thus the Muslims were included in St. Francis's worldview on mission, just as the Christians were included in the Muslim worldview on mission. Why is this important? It is important because St. Francis came into contact with the Sultan al-Kamil and the Muslims two years before his "Rule" was written. This is evidence that he was impressed by what he witnessed and learned firsthand about the Muslims. He was impressed so much so that his subsequent Rule went against the religious protocol of his day, a mission idea that emphasized the Crusade ideology that Muslims were served best with violence and war rather than the love of God.[34]

According to the Muslim Holy Book, the Qur 'ān:

> . . . Say: "It is not for me, of my own accord, to change it [the message of God], I follow naught but what is revealed unto me; if I were to disobey my Lord, I should myself fear the Penalty of a Great Day (to come). (x, 15)

St. Francis, like the Prophet Moḥammad, believed that it was his duty to deliver God's message to all people; and moreover, it was his duty to follow God's signs whether it pleased or displeased the people who preferred the Crusader notion of mission. It can be surmised then that the Sultan al-Kamil a devout follower of Prophet Moḥammad recognized the Muslim-like character of St. Francis. Such noble qualities in St. Francis made it easy for the Sultan al-Kamil to accept

---

[33]Marion A. Habig ed., *St. Francis of Assisi: Writings and Early Biographies - English Omnibus of the Sources for the Life of St. Francis* (Quincy, IL: Franciscan Press, 1991), 43-44.

[34]J. Hoeberichts, *Francis and Islam* (Quincy, IL: Franciscan Press, 1997), 45, 70; also see Habig, 21.

him on terms of endearment related to the spirituality of mission, rather than on terms based on enmity.[35]

St. Francis was a Good Muslim

. . . And nearest among them in love to the believers (Muslims) wilt thou find those who say, "We are Christians": Because amongst these are men devoted to learning and men who have renounced the world, and they are not arrogant.

And when they listen to the revelation received by the Apostle, thou wilt see their eyes overflowing with tears, for they recognize the truth: They pray: "Our Lord! We believe; write us down among the witnesses." (v. 85-86)

On his visit to the Muslims of Egypt [Damietta], St. Francis demonstrated his unique understanding of Christianity and his sincerity to it by his tolerance and appreciation of Islamic beliefs and virtues, though the public opinion of his day promoted the Islamic religion to be detestable in every respect. St. Francis, although a devout Christian, could still appreciate the Muslim point of view. For that reason, from the Islamic perspective, St. Francis was a Muslim at heart.[36] He was sincere, honest, devoted to learning, and, based on the Franciscan tradition, had truly renounced the fleeting and selfish ways of the world. Thus I want to emphasize both St. Francis's and the Sultan al-Kamil's notions of mission were one and the same. As a result, I can state the same idea about Prophet Moḥammad and St. Francis, that they are one in the spirituality of mission.

What is interesting about both of these great men, Prophet Moḥammad and St. Francis, is that although there are differences between them and their traditions, there are important basic similarities about the notion of God and humanity that unite them in the spirituality of mission. For both men, faith in God and his prescribed way for humanity was of ultimate concern. It can be stated then that regardless of the milieu that both men were born into, they chose a contemplative lifestyle, also called in both traditions a "prayerful

---

[35]Ali, 487.

[36]Ali, 268.

lifestyle." They both occupied themselves with God's presence in their lives.

Furthermore, according to the Franciscan tradition, "the will to live as in a hermit's cell [in the physical world] is a conscious choice of life."[37] Accordingly, both Prophet and Saint chose to live in a hermit's cell in the midst of a world of confusion and self-interest. The dynamic of faith operating in both their lives allowed for them to never become disillusioned by the ways of their societies, which could have resulted in a complete divorce from the world. Instead, they both chose and lived highly disciplined lives in the world for the sake of God.

Summary Conclusion

In sum, this study interpreting Prophet Moḥammad and St. Francis as Muslims of peace in the spirit of Mission can be further explained by looking at the responsibility that is placed on the shoulders of all Muslims. In Islam, the absence of any kind of priesthood or eccles-iastical organization such as formed in Christianity has caused the appearance of mission to be exhibited in forms very different from those that appear in the history of Christian mission. There are no missionary societies as such in Islam, and no specially trained agents. The only exception appears in the religious orders of Islam, whose organization resembles to some extent that of the monastic orders of Christianity. But even there, the absence of a priestly ideal and a theory separating the religious teacher from the common body of believers, creating the necessity of a special consecration and authorization to perform religious functions, makes for a fundamental difference in the two systems.

In Islam, the absence of a priestly class, specially set apart for the work of propagating the faith, is compensated for by the consequent feeling of responsibility resting on each individual believer. Because there is no intermediary between the Muslim and God, the responsibility for the Muslim's personal salvation rests on the believer alone. Consequently by default, the believer takes on a contemplative character by following strictly and carefully a performance of religious duties to God. As Prophet Moḥammad did, they use time wisely by

---

[37]Editorial Board, 10/1-2.

learning the requirements of the faith, thus becoming deeply impressed with the importance of their responsibilities to themselves and others. Such commitment elevates the faith of the believers to a higher level that incorporates faith and good deeds, called a missionary character in the presence of the non-Muslim. In which case, every Muslim is immersed in and exhibits the spirituality of mission.

Along these lines, side by side with the Imam [leader], the ulama [scholar], and mudarris [teacher] the annals of history of the Islamic religion contain the record of men and women of all ranks of society, from the sovereign to the peasant, and of all trades and professions, in the spirituality of mission. This is due to the universal character and conduct that is found in God's servants, such as Prophet Moḥammad and St. Francis of Assisi.

Lastly, for the sake of balance it would be necessary to show specifically how the spirituality of mission has worked in the Franciscan community as I have just demonstrated how it has worked in the Islamic community. But this study is not an exhausted one; so it is only necessary to posit that the Islamic ideas discussed in principle can serve for both traditions. This study has shown that there are greater similarities in both traditions than there are differences in the spirituality of mission.

I want to emphasize, however, that the Franciscan communities have imitated St. Francis's model of conduct, that is his Sunnah, and have internalized and openly practiced his ideas of the spirituality of mission from the beginning. Franciscan sources clearly reflect a rich tradition of practice and service. Hence the world, in every respect, is indebted to both Prophet Moḥammad and St. Francis for their belief in and conviction to the spirituality of mission in Islam and Franciscanism.

Bibliography

Ahsan, Muhammad Manazir. *Social Life Under the Abbasids: 170-289 AH (786-902 AD*, New York: Longman Group LTD, 1979.

Ali, Abdullah Yusuf. *The Holy Qur 'ān: Text, Translation and Commentary*. United States: Mcgregor & Werner, Inc., 1946.

Ali, Ameer. *A Short History of the Saracens*. Karachi: National Book Foundation, 1975.

Ali, Maulana Moḥammad. *The Religion of Islam: A Comprehensive Discussion of the Sources, Principles and Practices of Islam.* 3rd ed. Lahore: Ripon Printing, 1971.

Arnold, T.W. *The Preaching of Islam: A History of the Propagation of the Muslim Faith.* 2nd ed. London: Constable & Company LTD., 1913.

Corrigan, John., et al. *Jews Christians, Muslims: A Comparative Introduction to Monotheistic Religions.* New Jersey: Prentice Hall, 1998.

Cote, Richard G., O.M.I. *Re-Visioning Mission: The Catholic Church and Culture in Postmodern America.* New York: Paulist Press, 1996.

Cousins, Ewert. *Bonaventure: The Soul's Journey into God; the Tree of Life; the Life of St. Francis.* Trans. New York: Paulist Press, 1978.

Eaton, Richard M. *Islamic History as Global History.* Washington: American Historical Association, 1990.

Editorial Board. *Build with the Living Stones: a Program of Study on the Franciscan Missionary Charism.* 2nd ed. Silver Spring, Maryland: The Franciscan Mission Service, 1989.

Esposito, John L. *Islam: the Straight Path.* 3rd ed. New York: Oxford University Press, 1998.

—. *The Islamic Threat: Myth or Reality?* Revised. New York: Oxford, 1995.

Gabrieli, Francesco. *Arab Historians of the Crusades: Selected and Translated from the Arabic Sources.* London: Routledge & Kegan Paul, 1984.

Gibb, A.R. *Saladin: Studies in Islamic History.* Beirut: The Arab Institute for Research and Publishing, 1974.

Habig, Marion A., ed. *St. Francis of Assisi: Writings and Early Biographies: English Omnibus of the Sources for the Life of St. Francis.* Quincy IL.: Franciscan Press, 1991.

Haykal, Muhammad Husayn. *The Life of Muhammad.* 8th ed. United States: North American Trust Publications, 1976.

Hoeberichts, J. *Francis and Islam.* Quincy IL.: Franciscan Press, 1997.

Holt, P.M. *The Age of the Crusades: the Near East from the Eleventh Century to 1517.* New York: Longman Group, 1986.

Hopkins, Paul A. *What Next in Mission.* Philadelphia: The Westminster Press, 1977.

Hodgson, Marshall G. S. *The Venture of Islam: Conscience and History in a World Civilization.* Vol. 1 *The Classical Age of Islam.* Chicago: The University of Chicago Press, 1974.

—. *The Venture of Islam: Conscience and History in a World Civilization.* Vol. 2 *The Expansion of Islam in the Middle Periods.* Chicago: The University of Chicago Press, 1974.

Lazaro, Iriarte, O.F. M. *Franciscan History: The Three Orders of St. Francis of Assisi.* Chicago: Franciscan Herald Press, 1982.

Kedar, Benjamin Z. *Crusade and Mission: European Approaches toward the Muslims.* Princeton: Princeton University Press, 1984.

Lawrence, C.H, *The Frairs: The Impact of the Early Mendicant Movement on Western Society.* New York: Longman Group, 1994.

Maalouf, Amin. *The Crusades through Arab Eyes.* Trans. New York: Schocken Books, 1985.

Maier, Christoph T. *Preaching the Crusades: Mendicant Friars and the Cross in the Thirteenth Century.* Cambridge: Cambridge University Press, 1994

Paquette, François, O.F.M. Revised. *Islam and the Friars Minor.* Rome: International Franciscan OFM Commission, [ND].

Phipps, William E. *Muhammad and Jesus: A Comparison of the Prophets and their Teachings.* New York: Continuum Publishing Co., 1996.

Roncaglia Martiniano. *St. Francis of Assisi and the Middle East.* 3rd ed. Cairo: Franciscan Center of Oriental Studies, 1957.

Said, Edward W. *Orientalism.* New York: Vintage Books, 1979.

Sanneh, Lamin. *Translating the Message: the Missionary Impact on Culture.* Maryknoll, New York: 1989.

Short, William J. *The Franciscans.* 2nd vol. Wilmingon, Delaware: Michael Glazier Inc., 1989.

Sivan, Emmanuel. *Interpretations of Islam: Past and Present.* Princeton: The Darwin Press, 1985.

Breaking Down the Walls of Our Differences:
Islamic-Christian Encounter Through Prayer

François Paquette, O.F.M.

Nowadays, given the new technological conditions of our existence, rare are the people who can remain isolated. Exchanges of all kinds take place at a more and more accelerated pace. Individuals of minority groups settle for more or less long periods of time within indigenous majority populations. After staying a while, they either leave or settle for good in the new land. Their stay, whether temporary or permanent, gives them the opportunity not only to create ties with the host population but also to make their own culture and religious beliefs known. Exchange at the level of religious beliefs is perhaps the one most often absent, as if any such exchange would lead inevitably to proselytism and failure. Nevertheless, there exists a very non-threatening way of getting to know someone of another religion: by observing how they pray, and by reflecting on their prayer. This applies to a meeting between two people of different religions such as Islam and Christianity. One knows well that such a meeting takes place between two people and not between two religions and, therefore, one cannot disregard the social, cultural, political, economical, psychological and personal conditions in which each person evolves. In order to have a true inter-religious encounter, however, there must be an interaction of two people who are capable of situating themselves with respect to their own religion and who are spiritually inspired by their faith. Without this, the encounter would be bereft of a part essential to the dialogue, namely knowledge and experience of faith, and thus would not be fully realized.

The following chapter will be devoted to a presentation of the customs of prayer of two traditions, Islam and Christianity; the Catholic Christian tradition will be broached from the point of view of the Franciscan movement.[1] This presentation will be based on

---

[1] In Christianity there are several schools of thought and practice. Our focus is Catholic Christianity and, more specifically, in the Franciscan school, which is inspired by the way Francis of Assisi (1181-1226) lived his faith and which gave

the primary modes of prayer of the two traditions, those used in daily ritual and those associated with personal piety. Then follows a commentary revealing the parallels between Franciscan and Muslim ways of praying and a description of how Franciscans and Muslims may fraternize through prayer and show initiative in diminishing the gap which very often divides Islam and Christianity.

1.0 THE RITUAL PRAYER

Here it is not our intention to enter into a detailed description of these rites. Just enough information will be given to allow the reader to grasp the style, approach, and meaning of each. Various Christian and Franciscan sources will be used to present the modes of Franciscan prayers. As for the Muslim modes of prayer, they will be explained according to a synthesis taken from notes of Franciscan authors on their perception of Muslim prayers.[2]

1.1 Among the Muslims

The Muslim ritual prayer bears the name *salat* and is distinguished from the free prayer which is called *du'ā.'* The latter form of prayer does not involve any obligatory attitudes or formulas. The former, on the contrary, is meticulously regulated by religious law. It constitutes one of the most important duties for all Muslims, men and women, as soon as they attain the age of puberty. The children, without being strictly obligated, begin the practices at a very early age. Beginning at the age of reason, around seven years old, they are initiated and encouraged by their parents and their teachers. In practice, it is the city dwellers almost exclusively (though not necessarily all the city dwellers) who apply themselves to this daily duty of five ritual prayers. Obligatory, this prayer must, in fact, be carried out everyday (at dawn *(fajr)*, around mid-day *(zuhr)*, in the afternoon about three hours later *('asr)*, just after sunset *(maghrib)* and lastly when night has fallen *('isha')*. In order for this prayer to be valid, it should be preceded by ablutions, unless one is

---

birth to what is known today as the Franciscan family (Christians inspired by the spirituality of Francis of Assisi).

[2]Charles ABDel-Jalil, G. Basetti-Sani, *Mohammed et Saint-François* (Ottawa: Éd. Commissariat de Terre Sainte, 1959) 284.

already in a state of legal purity. This state is not in itself linked to sin; it is lost for example if one falls into a profound sleep, if one satisfies the slightest natural need, if one loses blood by natural or accidental causes, and the like.

The ablutions, an essential element of the Islamic prayer ritual, may be major or minor, according to the cause which led to the loss of legal purity. For major ablutions, it is necessary to apply a lotion to the entire body. For the other ablutions, it suffices to pour a little water on the hands, face, forearms, scalp, ears, neck, feet, and in the mouth and nostrils. When this is impossible, one places the hand on sand and makes a gesture as if to rub the different parts of the body.

The rites of this prayer as well as those of the preparatory ablutions are meticulously well-defined; any error in the accomplishment of these rites, even if inadvertant, renders the prayer invalid.

Before beginning, the believers face the *qibla* (the face turned towards Mecca), and express the intention to become apt to perform the prayer. Each one says:

In the name of Allah, the Clement, The Merciful! My God, I take refuge in You so that You save me from the presence of others.

O my soul. I beg Your pardon, O my God; and I convert and turn towards You. For You are He who loves to forgive; You are Merciful O my God, place me among those who profoundly convert; place me among those who purify themselves; place me among Your virtuous servants; make me a very patient and very grateful servant. Allow me to remember You and to name You often and to praise You morning and evening.

Each of the five daily prayers is composed of several *rakà* (a kind of unit of measure for prayer). The *rakà* is made up of a certain number of attitudes and gestures accompanied by formulas. The number of *rakà* varies according to the hours for the prayers; there may be two, three, or four obligatory *rakà*, never more. The entire daily prayer ends with a solitary *rakà* called *ouitr* which pious Muslims consider as the ultimate attestation of the Unique.

From the very first gesture of the prayer, the believers must consider themselves in a state of consecration in which they are set aside for God. They stand before Allah, in the presence of Allah; they speak to Allah. They must stay in this state until the end of the prayer and abstain from speaking, from looking around, from making the least gesture, and from saying the least word which has not been prescribed or authorized by religious law.

At the beginning of their prayer, the believers formulate the intention of performing such a prayer; they make a rather intricate gesture with their hands and arms while saying: *"Allah is Great!"* It is also recommended to add mentally the following formula (which is not, therefore, obligatory):

> *Allah is Great! Yes, He is Great. And to Him is given abundant praise. Glory to Him both morning and evening. I turn my face towards Him who created me; and I belong to those who give themselves to Him. Glory to You, O my God! And to Your praise! And blessed be Your Name! And exalted be Your Majesty! And powerful be Your glory! And there is no other Divinity than You!*

Recitation of the Qur 'ān: Each *rakà* includes the reciting of the first chapter of the Qur 'ān (which cannot be omitted) and another extract from this book. The choice of this extract is left to the believer who, however, must recite at least three verses. The pious believers choose chapters of variable lengths or a series of verses taken from a long chapter.

All the religious Islamic books also contain special collections. They contain notes relative to the choice of this passage from the Qur 'ān and to the preferences from which the believers have to take inspiration according to the different hours of the day, the times of the year and the personal situations in which they find themselves. Here are a few of the most widely used extracts: cf. Qur 'ān: The Fatiha, chap. 112; X, 129-130, 11, 256, XX1V, 35; L1X, 19-24.

The *ruku'*: After the recitation of the Qur 'ān, the believers bow down profoundly, until they are able to place their hands on their knees while keeping the back horizontal, and say, *"Allah is Great!"* They stay inclined the length of time it takes to say three times in a low voice, *"Glory to my Lord, the Immense! And to His praise!*" Then they rise saying, "*Allah hears those who praise Him! O Allah, our Master, to You the glory!*"

The *sujud* or prostration on the ground: This is the sign of the most perfect adoration which is due only to God. Islam protests all usage of this gesture towards creatures. The believers kneel and place the forehead and the palms of the hands on the ground and say, "*Allah is Great.*" They stay prostrated the time it takes to say three times, "*Glory to Allah and to His praise!*" Then they bend on their heels and say, "*Allah is Great!*" They prostrate again, saying the same formula as in the first prostration. While the believers are still crouched, they may say, "*O my God, forgive me; have mercy on me; take heed of my needs; guide me; and deliver me from my faults.*"

The *rakà* ends after the second prostration. Depending on the circumstances, one should get up and stand (after the first *rakà*) or then crouch again on the heels (if it is the second *rakà* or the final one). At the end of each prayer, the believers recite a formula called *tashahhud* (testimony).

Prayer conclusion: The believers turn to the right and, if there is someone there, to the left; the believers hail the angels and each other with these words, "*Peace be with you (al-salam 'alaykum),*" always in the plural, even if one is in the strictest of solitude.

The *qunūt* is a very venerable form of prayer. It must be recited at least once per day, in the last *rakà* of the night. This formula, partially or entirely, may have been part of the text of the Qur 'ān (where it is no longer found); this is a very ancient opinion.

1.2 Among the Franciscans

The Franciscan ritual prayer conforms to that of the Roman Catholic Church. It is comprised principally of the Divine Office and the Eucharist.

1.2.1   The Divine Office[3]

This name of Latin origin (*officium de facere*: to perform a service or function which one has to carry out) was given in the twelfth century to the great daily prayer of the Church, spread over

---

[3]M. Chebel, *Liturgy of the Hours* (New York: Catholic Book Publishing Co., 1975).

the entire day in order to sanctify time in its daily and annual routine. In this way it responded to the call of Christ, "Pray without ceasing,"[4] which the Vatican Council II strongly supports: "...in such a way that the day and night be sanctified by praise to God" (*Sacrosanctum Concilium*). By this Divine Office, the Church invites Christians to praise in union with all the people. This is the meaning behind the prayer, the "Hours," which, spread over the key moments of human life, symbolizes the continuous attention of Christians to the presence of God.[5]

The Church has always taken great care in the celebration of the "Hours" in which it sees a summit as well as a source of its spiritual life. This is why, on the one hand, it has organized the whole monastic life around this celebration and, on the other hand, it has asked the members of the clergy who do not belong to monastic orders to recite daily, under an abridged form, the Divine Office, formerly called the breviary, today called the Liturgy of the Hours or Prayer of Present Time.[6] Although the Divine Office is mostly prayed by religious orders, it is not theirs exclusively. All Christians are welcome to pray it.

The Divine Office unites us closely to God; it provides wise lessons of Christian and religious life. Besides the Psalms, it gives us the opportunity to read numerous passages from the Scriptures. The Psalms of the Divine Office exalt God's perfection; the Scripture lessons show its workings in the world, in the history of nations. The readings from the prophetic texts bring out God's design for the world's salvation and allow us to see with what wisdom God fulfills the design in time — the books linked to Christianity (texts from the New Testament, texts from the doctors of the Church or saints) unite with those of the Jewish tradition to instruct us about our duties and to reveal their wisdom.[7]

---

[4] Luke 18:1-8. All references to Sacred Scripture are taken from *The Jerusalem Bible*, Ed. Daron (London: Longman & Todd, 1960).

[5] M. Dubost, X. Lesort, S. Lalanne, V. Rouillard, *Théo., L'encyclopédie catholique pour tous* (Paris: Éd. Droguet, Ardant, Fayard, 1993) 940.

[6] M. Chebel, *Liturgie des Heures. Prière du temps présent* (Paris: Cerf-Desclée-Desclée de Brouwer-Mame, 1098; cf. Présentation de l'Office) XX-XL.

[7] Apollinaire de Saint Renan, pp. 122-125.

The Divine Office is made up of seven periods of prayer called "Hours"[8]: Office of Readings, Lauds, Tierce, Sext, None, Vespers and Compline. Only five among them are compulsory.[9] Matins, Tierce, and Sext, being optional, are recited mainly by monastic orders. Each one of the hours is composed of a hymn usually sung by all, a Psalm chanted in two choirs, followed by the doxology (*Glory be to the Father, the Son and the Holy Spirit as it was in the beginning, is now and ever shall be world without end. Amen*) and a reading from the Bible. Over the centuries, these essential elements have always been in effect. Secondary elements have been added to help enter into prayer: titles and antiphons (short phrases taken from Biblical texts) for the Psalms, responsories after the readings (short praises), acclamations, and refrains which serve to manifest the community in prayer, verses of introduction and conclusion.[10]

The contents of the Divine Office vary according to the hour of the day. The prayers are divided according to liturgical times in such a way as to highlight the celebrations (Christmas, Easter, Sanctorals, etc.), to remember the deceased, and to praise God for the benefits of creation. The type of community celebration varies in function of the degree of solemnity, the possibilities and dimensions of the assembly, and the style demanded by each Hour, such as a particular degree of solemnity, a more meditative aspect, or a celebration by small groups or in private. Silence is an essential element of the celebration. This explains why it is placed normally after the texts to permit interiorization of the Word. In the Office, a physical attitude accompanies the prayer. One is sometimes standing, seated, or in prostration according to the importance accorded to the text. It is preferable that the Office be said in a group, but it can also be said in private. In this case, the prayer demands a certain adaptation: omitting certain elements which imply a dialogue with the assembly (repetition in the responsories,

---

[8] Because it divides the day to remind one to render thanks to the Creator.

[9] Canon 1174-1178, in John–Paul II, *Cathéchisme de l'Église Catholique* (Ottowa: Éd. Conférence des Évêques catholiques du Canada [CECC], 1993) 676.

[10] M. Dubost, X. Lesort, S. Lalanne, V. Rouillard, *Théo., L'encyclopédie catholique pour tous* (Paris: Éd. Droguet, Ardant, Fayard, 1993) 940.

final benediction, and monition at the beginning of the intercession).[11]

Since the very beginning of the Order, the Franciscans have taken up the habit of praying the Divine Office as a group.[12] The Office is for them a sign of fraternity which should express the internal unity of all the brothers and their union with the Church.[13] This union was to be guaranteed above everything else. To prove it, Francis of Assisi said of the brothers who did not adhere to the Office that "he considered them neither Catholics nor his brothers."[14] Also in these writings Francis of Assisi established a strong bond between saying the Office and being Catholic[15] — the Office was a means of reinforcing their will to be faithful to God. When reciting the Office, Franciscans enter into a real and invisible communion with the Church; their prayer spreads to the four corners of the world.[16]

Today a certain flexibility is given to the way in which the Divine Office is recited. Although it is recommended that the brothers follow the prescribed protocol established by the Catholic Church, creativity is encouraged in the manner of preparing and experiencing this time of prayer.

1.2.2 The Eucharist

The Eucharist, from the Greek for thanksgiving, signifies thanksgiving, praise, joy. This very ancient appellation originates in

---

[11] A.-G. Martimort, et. al. *L'Église en prière. Introduction à la liturgie.* 3e Ed. (Paris: Desclée Co., 1965) 158-159.

[12] The Rule of 1223, ch. 3, nn. 1-3, in Maion Habig, et. al., *St. Francis of Assisi. Writing and early biographies; English Omnibus of the Sources for the Life of St. Francis,* Ed. Marion A. Habig, (Quincy, IL: Franciscan Press, 1972) 59–60; (Hereafter referred to as *Omnibus*); General Constitution of the Order of Friars Minor, § 23.3, in H. Schaluck, *Règle et Constitutions générales de l'Ordre des Frères Mineurs* (Paris: Éd. Franciscaines, 1991) 155. (Here after referred to as CCGG).

[13] M. Hubaut, Éd., *La voie franciscaine* (Paris: Desclée de Brouwer, 1983) 67.

[14] Letter to the Entire Order, n. 44, in *Omnibus*, 107.

[15] Testament of St. Francis, n. 30-31, in *Omnibus*, 69.

[16] M. Chebel, *L'esprit d'oraison et de dévotion. Thème d'approfondissement et de réflexion.* Secrétariat général OFM pour la Formation et les Études (Rome: Curie générale des Frères Mineurs, 1996) 83.

a Jewish ceremony.[17] It is a meal where God makes alliance with the participants. This alliance, which recalls that of the Old Testament, is addressed in a new and definitive way to all mankind. On the eve of his Passion, Jesus had celebrated the Jewish Passover with his disciples. During this meal he took the bread and, rendering thanks to God, he blessed it, broke it, and gave it to his disciples, saying[18], "Take and eat of this, all of you, for this is my body given for you." Similarly, after the meal he took the cup and, giving thanks to God, he blessed it and gave it to his disciples, saying, "Take and drink of this, all of you, for this is the cup of my blood, the blood of the new and eternal alliance, which will be shed for you and for all the multitude, in forgiveness of sins. You will do this in memory of me."[19]

Thus during the Eucharist, Christians implore God for the forgiveness of their sins, they pray for one another, they render thanks to God by a Psalm and chants, they listen together to texts from the Bible and to a lesson and commentary on the texts they read (homily). They commemorate the death and resurrection of Jesus and they celebrate the meal where Christ rendered himself present and where still today he renders himself to the one who eats the bread and drinks from the cup of shared wine.[20] All Franciscans who live or find themselves in the same place celebrate the Eucharist everyday as a group, in such a way that the Eucharist is truly the center and the source of all brotherly communion.[21]

---

[17] Ceremony taken from the Vigil of Passover where each Israelite family thanks God for their liberation and for other spiritual freedoms of which this initial ceremony is the sign. The order is the same as the Eucharist celebrated today: remembrance of the great things God has done for people; songs and thanksgivings; blessing of bread and the cup and the sharing of the bread and sometimes the cup. See Dubost, 953.

[18] The words of consecration used in the Eucharistic celebration.

[19] 1Cor. 11:23-26; Mt. 26:26-29; Lk. 22:15-20.

[20] Dubost, 958-969.

[21] Letter to the Entire Order, n. 12.30.33, in *Omnibus*, 102-106; CCGG 21.2.

1.3 The Call to Prayer

1.3. 1   Among the Muslims

At the hour of prayer, the muezzin climbs up the minaret and proclaims the call to prayer; this is the *adhān* (the word muezzin comes from *mu 'adhdhin*, the one who does the *adhān*). One should not confuse the muezzin with the imam, who presides over the prayer and directs it when it is carried out in a group. The imam must be a person of knowledge and of piety. The muezzin has a less important function which demands much less knowledge. Both are lay people, just like the other believers.

In the Orient, the call to prayer is chanted; in the Maghreb it is more or less chanted with an extension of the ends of the phrases and with long pauses. Many European Franciscans living in North-African regions[22] have remarked upon the strange charm or the strong religious impression of these human voices calling the believers to leave their temporal activities and to turn entirely towards the All Powerful. Here is the formula of the *adhān*:

> *Allah is Great (four times or twice, according to the school of Law)*
> > *2. I proclaim there is no other divinity than Allah (repeat)*
> > *3. I proclaim that Moḥammad is the Messenger of Allah (repeat)*
> > *4. Hasten to the prayer (repeat)*
> > *5. Hasten to the bliss (repeat)*
> > *6. Allah is Great (repeat)*
> > *7. There is no other Divinity than Allah.*

During the *adhān*, the believers should collect themselves, lend their ears and repeat after the muezzin in a low voice the elements of the call, except for four and five which are replaced by the following formula so often employed by the Muslims: "*There is no strength nor power but through Allah.*" When the *adhān* is over, it is recommended that the believers say the following prayer:

> *O my God and Lord, it is the perfect call! It is the time of prayer! Give to Moḥammad the credit and the merit and supreme rank; and make him appear (on the day of the resurrection) in a*

---

[22] Those from the Maghreb.

situation of excellence which You have promised him. You are He who never fails to keep His promise.

1.3.2   Among the Franciscans

1.3.2.1 The Bells

To bring the faithful together for the liturgy, several means more or less primitive have been adapted during the first centuries: certain Oriental Churches have remained faithful to the blocks of wood or *siderun*, hanging pieces which one hits with a mallet. The use of bells appeared towards the end of the fifth century. The ritual which surrounds it at the time shows that one expects from the bell more than a simple summoning of the faithful; it is a kind of sacred ritual to which the prayer of the Church gives a power to chase away demons and misfortunes.[23] Finally, its use developed to invite the absent faithful to come together to pray in the liturgy — hence the sound of bells in the midst of the celebration — and also to encourage private moments of prayer as in the case of bells for the Ave Maria and the Angelus.[24] It would also accentuate the parish life announcing baptisms, mariages, deaths, funerals, fire. In some places the tolling of bells announces fire, war, situations of emergency.

1.3.2.2 The Call to Prayer

In the writings of Francis of Assisi, there are two passages underlining the call to prayer. The first comes from the Letter to the Custodians[25] (i.e., those responsible for the local or regional communities)(v. 8) sent between 1220-1224, stating:

Teach and preach to all peoples this duty to praise Him, so that at every hour and at the sound of the bells, praise and thanksgiving be always rendered, by all the people and all over the earth, to God Almighty.

---

[23] Dubost, 639.

[24] The first is a salutation to Mary and a prayer asking her to intercede for the supplicant. The second recalls events surrounding the birth of Jesus, each one accompanied by a short intercession.

[25] *Omnibus, 113.*

The second is drawn from the Letter to the chiefs of the nations[26] (v. 7), written, without a doubt in Syria in 1220, at which time Francis of Assisi heard again the call to the prayer by the muezzin:

Each evening, have proclaimed by a town crier or give warning by some other signal that all should render praise and thanks to the Lord God Almighty.

Even if the bells were already used in certain Benedictine monasteries, we may feel here a certain nostalgia for the prayers at dawn and at sunset in the Muslim camp. One may assume that the brothers were called to prayer by a crier, which may be an echo of the meeting of Francis and the Sultan.[27] Today, be it either by the muezzin or by the ringing of bells, Muslims and Franciscans find in this call not only an invitation to prayer but also an invitation to abandon their worldly activity in order to turn to God and unite their prayer to praise God.

1.4 The Place of Prayer

1.4.1 Among the Muslims

The place of prayer for the Muslims is very sacred. It involves a separate space. There are three kinds: those where major religious events are commemorated, those where Islamic worship is usually celebrated, and the Qur 'ān itself as sacred writing. There are also three sacred locations where only Muslims in a state of ritual purity are admitted: Mecca, Medina, and a Muslim section in the city of Jerusalem. The mosque is also a place reserved for Muslims in a pure state where one has to be barefoot to enter. Muslims make a distinction between al-jāmi, the mosque where the assembly meets for the Friday prayer, and the *al-masjid*, the simple neighborhood oratory. The mosque has, besides a space reserved for prayer, socio-cultural areas. However, far from being reserved only for the mosque, the prayer may be said in all places where Muslims find themselves when the muezzin does the call.

---

[26] *Omnibus, 116.*

[27] G. Jeusset, *Rencontre sur l'autre rive, François d'Assise et les Musulmans* (Paris: Éd. Franciscaines, 1996) 137.

1.4.2   Among the Franciscans

The Church is the sacred building dedicated to divine worship with a view to be used by all the faithful in public.[28] If they use or construct buildings, these are not temples, but houses destined to reunite the congregation of prayer. The architectural styles that one can see are not only conveniences, but they express diverse spiritual concepts according to countries and times. Traditionally, the building was decorated in such a way as to give a festive atmosphere to the assembly and to the celebration. The figurative decorations — the frescos, mosaics, sculptures, and stained glass — contribute to this festive atmosphere, but aim to be an extension of the signs themselves, underlining notably the celestial aspect of the liturgy. That is why the iconographic themes cannot be left to chance. It is in these places with an altar that the Franciscans celebrate the Divine Office. They thus try to avoid all exterior disturbances during this celebration.[29] Christians identified with Christ by their baptism are also the temples of the Holy Spirit. That is why the place of prayer for the Franciscans is not only the cloister or the choir. They have to learn to pray among ordinary workers, the poor, and the sick showing people that the inner life is not reserved only for monks and priests but for all.

1.5 The body at Prayer

In all the elements of human life whether we like it or not, it is impossible to make abstraction of the body. It is the body which places us in relation with the world. Everything that man does demands action on the part of the body. Thus the prayer is expressed by the lips, through corporeal attitudes, and by gestures, all of which are not left to free expression but are determined by religious laws. The unanimity of hearts expresses itself at least as much as by attitudes of the body as by words, by chants.[30] Bodily expression is a particularly important way of participating actively in

---

[28] Canon 1159-1162.

[29] K. Esser, *Origines et Objectifs primitifs de l'Ordre des Frères Mineurs.* (Paris: Éd. Franciscaines, 1983; Leiden: Trad. de l'allemand par E.J. Brill, 1966) 130, 7.

[30] A.–G. Martimort, et al. *L'Église en prière. Introduction à la liturgie.* 3e Ed. (Paris: Desclée et Co., 1965) 747.

prayer. It is also a way of expressing the spiritual unanimity of the assembly.

1.5.1   Among the Muslims

The *sujud*, or ground prostration, is the sign of most perfect adoration which is due to God alone. It has to be done with seriousness and is intended to be a sign of submission before Allah.

The seated position is the position of receptiveness, alertness, and attention on the part of the students before their teacher. As the majority of Muslim places of prayer do not have any facilities for sitting, all usually sit on the floor.

In the standing position the students express their respect by presenting themselves before Allah.

1.5.2   Among the Franciscans

Kneeling is considered by the brothers as penitential, a sign of mourning, of humility, of repentance, characterizing the fast where one kneels for certain prayers. It is equally the privileged attitude of individual prayer although not obligatory. It still expresses supplication, submission, repentance, dependence, and adoration.

The seated position is the attitude of those who listen.[31] It is also a position favorable to collecting one's thoughts and to meditation.

Bowing is a substitution for genuflection and is associated with a time of reflection.

The standing position is first of all, in its natural sense, a sign of respect. One usually stands in front of a person that one wishes to honor. We recall, when we are standing for prayer, the day commemorating the resurrection and the grace which has been given to us, but we are also reminded of the fact that this day is in some way the image of the century to come.[32] This position also recalls that of a tree, that of a free person, living, standing before God.[33] Prostration was used more frequently in the past as a way of venerating God.

---

[31] Martimort, 747.
[32] Martimort, 747.
[33] Dubost, 942.

In the beginning of the Order, the Divine Office had to be prayed standing at the prescribed hour.[34] Today, different positions may be adopted during the course of the prayer. Franciscan spiritual movements have contributed over the last years to restoring the importance of the role of the body in prayer. Without a minimum of appropriate arrangements, the body is a hindrance to prayer, whereas on the contrary, it could be a help, provided one uses these resources.[35]

Other gestures that are specifically Christian creations: the sign of the Cross,[36] the kiss of peace, the beating the chest in sign of penitence, the hands raised and extended to remember Jesus on the Cross. No matter the gesture, it should be accompanied in a way to be seen and understood, while remaining modest and free from sentimentality.

1.6 Moments of Prayer

1.6.1   Among the Muslims

After the ritual prayer, it is recommended to make invocations before withdrawing. This is the *dhikr* (mention and remembrance of the name of Allah) which becomes a methodical exercise in the religious fraternities. It is very praiseworthy to say *"Glory to Allah"* thirty-three times; *"Praise to Allah"*, the same number of times; and *"Allah is Great,"* equally thirty-three times. The number one hundred will be attained, by adding the formula which is so fundamental: *"There is no other Divinity than Allah; the Unique; without associate."*

The Muslims, with the exception of men at midday on Friday, are not held to make their prayers in the mosque in common. However the prayer of the "assembly" (*jamā 'a)*— which is a more collective one — is strongly recommended for each hour of the day, even the earliest. Many pious believers follow this advice. When it is performed in a group, the prayer is presided by an imam who

---

[34] 2Celano n. 96, in *Omnibus*, 441-442.

[35] Dubost, 748.

[36] Tracing on the body the sign of cross. One places the hand on the forehead saying, "In the Name of the Father," then on the chest saying, "In the Name of the Son", then on the left shoulder saying, "In the Name of the Spirit," and finally on the right shoulder saying, "Amen."

stands at the front, at the entrance to the alcove arranged for this in the wall of the mosque. The believers who are present place themselves behind the imam, in orderly rows (the muezzin reminds them, crying in the midst of the faithful: *"Souou couufoufakoume yarhamkoum Allah"* — *"Get in line and may God have mercy on you"*). When the prayer begins, the believers make the same gestures as the imam, without being obliged to recite all the formulas, but to be attentive to the hours when the imam must recite them in a loud voice. The imams are charged with not making the prayer too long and not to impose their personal piety on the group of believers present behind them.

1.6.2   Among the Franciscans

Everyday, the brothers are invited to praise God, but Sunday remains the festive day, that which is reserved for the celebration of the resurrection of Jesus. Normally, work activities are reduced, and the day is devoted principally to praising God.

1.7 Other Votive Prayers

1.7.1   The Chaplet

1.7.1.1 Among the Muslims

For their invocations Muslims use the chaplet of ninety-nine beads corresponding to the different names or attributes given to God in the Qur'ān (the hundredth name will be revealed in heaven).

1.7.1.2 Among the Franciscans

The Franciscan "crown" originates from the chaplet.[37] The Franciscan chaplet is composed of seven series of ten beads. The recitation consists of reciting one Ave Maria per bead; each series of ten begins by a Pater (prayer of praise, thanksgiving, and pardon addressed to God) and the recitation of the Gospel, accompanied by

---

[37]The Chaplet is normally made up of five series of ten beads, each series followed by a separated bead. A rosary corresponds to the recitation of three chaplets.

a brief commentary on an event in the life of Mary and Jesus, concluding with a Gloria (doxology, cf 1.2.1).

1.7.2   Fasting

1.7.2.1 Among the Muslims

The one who fasts *(siyam* or *ṣwan)* becomes able to support the trials of life and becomes attentive to the fate of those most in need. The Islamic fast consists of total abstinence from nourishment (both solid and liquid) and from sexual relations. The fast begins a little before dawn and ends at sunset *(maghrib)*. Islam acknowledges three kinds of fasts: the fast of Ramadan, obligatory for the whole community; the periodic fast, voluntary at other moments of the year or on special days of the week (Monday and Thursday); and the fast to obtain pardon for sins. The one who voluntarily breaks the fast commits a fault which has to be expiated. By fasting, Muslims translate into action the spiritual, moral, and social prescriptions of Islam. This is a form of solidarity with the poor: "Those who sleep with a full stomach while their neighbor is suffering from hunger are not believers *(ḥadith).*" Although it is an act of personal asceticism, it is also a collective and public testimony stressing the fact that one is here on earth in order to submit oneself to God.[38]

1.7.2.2 Among the Franciscans

Christ invited his disciples to fast without display[39] and he himself fasted.[40] In turn, the Apostles fasted[41] and in the early Church Wednesdays and Fridays have also been considered as days of fasting (there are traces of this practice in the beginning of the first century). One prepared for Easter by fasting. Today the Catholic Church prescribes fasting only twice per year — Ash Wednesday (beginning of Lent) and Good Friday (commemoration of the death of Jesus) — but encourages practices of renouncement and sharing. St. Francis of Assisi says:

---

[38] Dubost, 143.
[39] Mt. 6:16.
[40] Mt. 4:2.
[41] Acts 13:2; 14:23; 2Cor. 11:27.

The brothers will fast from the Feast of All Saints to Christmas. Concerning the holy Lent which begins at the Epiphany and lasts for forty consecutive days, and which Our Lord has made sacred by his holy fast, those who wish to observe it, may they be blessed by the Lord; and those who do not, they are not compelled. All, on the contrary, must fast during the other fast which lasts until the Resurrection of the Lord. For the rest of the year, the brothers are not obliged to fast except on Fridays. In case of necessity, the brothers are not held to corporeal fast.[42]

Today the brothers practice fasting by taking a meal without meat and alcohol or by reducing their consumption to bread and water. The most fervent abstain from eating altogether.

1.8 Pilgrimages

1.8.1 Among the Muslims

The pilgrimage to Mecca is the fifth pillar of Islam.[43] The Muslim tradition presents Mecca as the world's axis and the place where one recalls the story of Abraham. The pilgrimage rites allow Muslims to enter into a spiritual rebirth. If one has the financial means, it is obligatory. It must take place within the three lunar months at the end of the year, but the official *Hajj* takes place between the seventh and the tenth of the month, *Dhu-I-hijja*. The pilgrimage is very important to give concrete expression to the Umma, the fraternity of believers of all colors. The prayers aid in reflection and the gathering together favors a sense of strength and unity. A small individual pilgrimage may be made any time during the year: the *'umra*, which consists of doing a part of the rites of *Hajj*, called the *Tawāf* (seven strolls around the *Ka 'ba*), and the seven hikes between the two little hills, *Safa* and *Marwa*.[44]

---

[42] 2R3. 5-9, in *Omnibus*, 60.

[43] It is in this way that the Muslims identify the five obligations which fundamentally resume the religious and cultural practice: the profession of faith, prayer, fasting, alms, and pilgrimage. See J.-R. Milot, *L'islam et les musulmans* (Québec: Éd. Fides, 1993) 76.

[44] Surate 22, The Qurān.

Summary of *Ḥajj:*

The seventh of the month is the sermon by the Qadis of Mecca near the *Ka 'ba* that the Muslims go around. On the eighth they go to Minā, one of the places of Abraham where they pass the night as Moḥammad did. On the ninth they go to Mount Arafāt from noon to the evening where they stand before God. Then they go to Muzdalifa where they collect seven pebbles and spend the night in prayer. On the nineteenth, at dawn, they return to Minā with the seven pebbles which they throw as a sign of the lapidation of Satan. Then the great sacrifice takes place, a commemoration of the sacrifice of Abraham.[45]

1.8.2 Among the Franciscans

The Stations of the Cross: Ever since the beginning of the fourth century, crowds of Christians each year have wanted to be in Jerusalem during the week of the Passion of Christ and to retrace the path which Jesus followed during the hours which preceded his death. In a certain way they wanted to relive the event, to identify themselves with Jesus and, by this gesture, to offer him thanks.

Ten centuries later, Franciscans created and spread a devotion called "The Stations of the Cross." As Keepers of the Holy places since the fourteenth century, in accordance with an agreement with the Turks, they directed the spiritual exercises of the pilgrims on the Via Dolorosa, taken by Christ on his way to Pilate's tribunal, from the base of the city up to the summit of Golgotha (Calvary). They had the idea of transferring this form of meditation on the Passion into the framework of the everyday life of the faithful and, in this way, allowing the poor and those who could not travel to the Holy Land to carry out the same procedure as the pilgrims. In order to do this, they set up outside or in churches a series of statues, paintings, or crosses recalling scenes marking stages of Christ's route to Calvary. They encouraged prayers and meditations of the faithful at each one of these steps or "stations."[46]

---

[45] Taken from F. Paquette, *L'islam et les frères mineurs*, Ed. International Franciscan Commission for Relation with the Muslims [IFCRM], (Rome) 65-66.

[46] The number of stations varied and in 1958 it became customary to construct fourteen stations and to end this pilgrimage with a prayer to Mary, mother of Jesus. See Martimort, 747-749.

Other varied forms of pilgrimage exist among the Franciscans: several around the cult of Francis of Assisi, the founder,[47] and of other saints of the Franciscan family, and others in connection with particular themes or places (for example, peace-walks; pilgrimages to the Holy Land).

For Muslims, pilgrimages efface personal sins but they are also a strong expression of the common faith of believers in their diversity. For the Franciscans, they are a moment of searching for an identity which is found in returning to the sources of Christianity or of Franciscan history and in affirming a faith that is evolving.

Ritual prayer occupies a great place in the Muslim religion. The forms just elucidated determine a religious attitude dominated by the greatness of God, sovereign, absolute and inaccessible, unique Master of the destiny of all creatures. Muslims owe God adoration and praise, submission, and obedience. They expect rewards from God's liberality and fear punishments from God's incomparable justice. Recognizing God's oneness and absolute transcendence, they may hope for everything through God's mercy. Ritual prayer is a form of discipline that the Franciscans use to encounter God in order to praise, and invoke God, and to implore God's pardon in a brotherly way. Whether it be Muslims or Franciscans, it offers them a means of giving themselves time, space, words, and gestures to affirm their faith and show their belonging to a religious group.

Beyond ritual prayer, other more personal forms of prayers exist among Muslims and Franciscans and depend on the availability and the rhythm of each person. The intent of the following section is to reveal some of these.

2.0 PERSONAL OR PRIVATE PRAYER

2.1 Among the Muslims

Ritualism seems to dominate official Islam. Among the canonists, there is even a tendency to exclude all other forms of religion. The rites must not only be sufficient for believers, but also be the unique channel for piety among the most ardent: the supererogatory itself has to be modeled on the obligatory rites and

---

[47]CCGG 26, 2-3.

to reproduce them. Any addition can be rejected as an innovation (*bid'a*) that alters the purity of the religion. This is obedience, submission (islam).

Personal piety, duā, has been developed most often by reference to the indications found in the Qur 'ān and to the examples that, according to tradition, hark back to the time of the Prophet and his companions. It remains quite ritualistic. It puts to work, however, certain elements of "interior" religion that are authentically Muslim, preserved in the Qur 'ān and the Sounna and to which the ritual prayer does not give full value.

2.1.1 Supererogatory Prayers

Other than the five ritual prayers which are a daily duty for every Muslim, the Qur 'ān and the Sounna recommend more or less clearly the prayer which is recited during the night *(tahajjud)* or added by personal devotion to the obligatory prayers (*nāfila*, plural: *nawāfil*). These supererogatory prayers reproduce the attitudes, gestures, and formulas of the ritual prayers. The same spirit of adoration, fear, supplication, and hope reigns, but they are taken over by personal devotion, as an exercise of asceticism and of religion that is not imposed. Among these prayers are those said at night during the month of Ramadan, the *tarâouih*, which, in the illuminated mosques, contribute to giving a serene intensity to the fervor of the pious believers.

2.1.2 Meditation on the Qur 'ān

The book of Allah is considered by the Muslims as the textual word of God, dictated to the messenger through the intermediary of an angel or by interior revelation. Without going as far as deifying the letters, the sounds, the ink, and the paper which were used in the recitation on the text (as a few ancient literalists had overzealously taught), the Muslims profess a veneration for the Qur 'ān. While they are reading, copying or reciting it, they have the impression that they are entering into a most intimate contact with God. The Word of Allah (*kalam*) is like a special presence of the Most High at the moment when it is pronounced.

When it is not simply a literal recitation, destined to fulfill a kind of performance (for example, that of running through the sacred text in a certain lapse of time — one day, three days, one week), the devotion shown for the Qur'ān goes beyond ritualism and contributes to piety and to religiousness as a whole, a real greatness and a certain sense of the hidden mystery of God and the work of God. It stimulates thoughtful minds to meditation and to a greater attention to the presence and the action of the Unique. Many Muslims reach the point where they express their most profound sentiments before God and before everyone only by the verses of the Qur'ān assimilated through repetition and meditation.

2.1.3   Other Personal Prayers

A certain number of prayer formulas pass into pious usage before all others. These are the formulas that the Muslim tradition traces back to Moḥammad himself. Collections have been made to guide the believers in their choice and to guarantee the authenticity of these prayers that piety believes are more effective because they have come from the messenger of Allah who used them frequently himself. They often find their place at the end of the ritual prayer but also at other moments and most believers repeat them unaltered with a spirit of faith in the blessing (tabarruk) attached to the examples and works of the Prophet.

Little by little, however, other formulas of prayer, attributed to the most reputable people for their "faithfulness to God," have been introduced in the collective piety of the Muslims. They express needs and aspirations that the mold of ritual and para-ritual piety leaves unsatisfied.

Without exception, these formulas remain fairly poor. If they provoke a certain religious emotion, this is due mainly to texts borrowed from the Qur'ān, introduced and arranged in a predictable manner. Certain formulas from the Shiites have nevertheless a poignant tone and express a sincere and profound piety. It would be worthwhile to make a special study of this.

2.2 Among the Franciscans

Among the Franciscans, Francis of Assisi asks the brothers to pray using the Divine Office and the celebration of the Eucharist but also through meditation and the orison to which the Franciscans devote themselves everyday either in private or as a community.[48] They apply themselves to the reading and meditating of the Holy Gospel and other texts (Bible) showing a great veneration towards them.[49] The meditation consciously has recourse to thought and mental images. The practitioners recall a word, a scene from the Gospel or a point of Christian faith on which they reflect. They picture in their imagination how things came to pass. They reflect about the deep meaning of such words, why they were said, to whom, etc. They gain from this a deeper view of the words or reported circumstances and this reflection sustains and enriches their spiritual and moral life. There are other ways in which reason and will may intervene in meditation — by imagining the presence of God in oneself and seeking always to imbue oneself more in it. The meditation is active through thought and acts consciously. Meditation precedes contemplation where the "I" renders itself more passive and frees itself of all reflection or voluntary consideration in order to remain in silence before God.

The orison is an extended prayer. There is less room for reflection and more for the impulses of the heart and the will. These become simpler of themselves; the orison then becomes a silent presence before God. The believers humbly open themselves to the mysterious action of the spirit of God which works in the heart of all people. The orison may be accompanied by joy, by an overwhelming peace, but it is often a pure attitude of faith which holds steady before a God who remains a mystery. This form of prayer is not reserved for sages or scholars. Because it is a gift of God, it may arise in the hearts of all who believe and seek. The orison occupies an important part in the life of the Franciscans. As St. Francis said, "May the brothers never lose the spirit of orison and may they pray without ceasing."[50]

---

[48] CCGG 24.

[49] CCGG 22.

[50] 1R22,29, in *Omnibus*, 49.

For the Franciscans, there exists a strong relation between the faithful practice of personal orison and the realization of the religious life itself. By consecrating a precise moment of the day to interior prayer, in order to live the personal rapport with God, the brother, like a monk, nourishes devotion to God. If this practice is bound to be regular, it is because St. Francis insists on the daily commitment of the brother and of the fraternity to reserve a time favorable to personal orison in order to live in the spirit of orison and devotion. This faithfulness becomes a means of deepening faith - finding strength in God to face the challenges of each day.[51]

The time for meditation has to be left to our disposition in order to better understand the Word of God and to integrate this Word into our personal and community life. The first goal of this time, reserved for an intimate union with the Lord, is to reach a spiritual knowledge of God in Christ and to better discern God's will for each brother and for the growth of the whole fraternity.[52]

Personal or private prayer leaves room for other forms of prayer in which the believers speak to God in terms which are not strictly imposed by religious laws, in terms which are open to their own creativity and which correspond to their own personality. These leave place for mystical prayer, a prayer in which the soul speaks to God, the heart opens and prepares itself before the greatness and sings the desire of union which in itself is a reflection of intimacy.

In this outline of ritual and personal Islamic and Franciscan prayer, the principal modes of prayer were only briefly described. The aim was to introduce some of the main forms of prayer and some of the formulas which accompany them. The aim was not to discuss any aspects where one religion may have influenced the other. At the beginning of the Order, Francis of Assisi wrote very little before his departure for the East. It is thus almost impossible to establish a comparison between the texts redacted before and those redacted after his trip. In the life of St. Francis of Assisi, however, as well as in the lives of the Franciscans who followed him throughout the centuries, we have seen that it is possible to draw certain parallels, not at the level of faith as such but in the manner of practicing it. The section which follows will reveal what appear

---

[51] Chebel, *L'esprit d'oraison et de dévotion*, 88-89.
[52] Chebel, 88-89.

to us to be a few interesting Franciscan initiatives in the area of dialogue through prayer.

3.0 INTERRELIGIOUS INITIATIVES

Many are the Franciscans who have sought and found ways of uniting their efforts to those of the Muslims to offer themselves to the service of humanity. These links have been knit through many different works: charitable works include dispensaries set up and directed by both Muslims and Franciscans. In education, in several countries, schools attended by both Muslims and Christians have both Muslims and Franciscans as teachers. Social works such as orphanages and community centers to help people find lodging, food, clothing and jobs, are also directed by both Muslims and Franciscans. In several places where Muslims and Franciscans collaborate there is daily dialogue. It strengthens bonds, diminishes prejudices, changes perceptions, reduces fears, and invites the other to meet at a deeper level.

Besides these occasions for dialogue, the brothers have realized that prayer is also a favorable ground for mutual respect. As we have noted, the forms of prayer show parallels in that they try to express a collective and singular bond of human beings before God. Be it either by ritual or personal prayer, all aim to praise and implore God.[53] In several countries where Franciscans live in a majority Muslim population, the brothers have sought means of solidarity with Muslims through prayer. The following lines aim to convey some of them and show how these initiatives may contribute to build a society at once pluralistic and respectful of religious differences.

3.1 The Call to Prayer and the Recitation of the Divine Office

The Muslim times for prayers are established according to the solar and lunar calendar. The Christian prayer of the Divine Office is also regulated by the solar calendar. Consequently, the muezzin's chant and the church bells often occur at the same time to call Muslims and Franciscans to prayer. In certain towns in the Magreb,

---

[53] Surate 29, The Qur`ān.

the brothers do not ring the church bells for the call to prayer at midday. They accept the first notes of the muezzin's chant as a sign that it is time to pray to God. In some Franciscan fraternities, the brothers pray in Arabic and add to the doxology the expression "Unique God" to signify that the God of Christians and that of Muslims is not different but can be understood differently.

3.2 The Place of Worship

It is not rare that a Christian place of worship be frequented by a Muslim. In Morocco, for example, a prayer room at the convent of the Poor Clare sisters close to the Franciscan monastery is frequently visited by Muslim women who come on occasion to reflect. Sometimes Franciscans go to Mosques to visit their imam friends and they take advantage of the occasion to perform short personal devotions to God. For these Franciscans and Muslims, personal prayer goes beyond the physical and religious framework. It cannot be restricted to a place. On the other hand, Muslim artists have collaborated on the decoration of the chapel of the Franciscan sisters of Casablanca by offering two statues sculpted in wood; the first represents St. Francis of Assisi, the other St. Clare of Assisi. This gesture invited the Franciscans to offer, in turn, to a mosque of the village of Agouim in Morocco, a wooden chair sculpted by a brother. It is currently used by the imam during Friday prayer. These initiatives demonstrate well the respect held by both for the other's place of worship.

3.3 Fasting

Several Franciscans start the fast of the Christian Lent early to coincide with Ramadan and they extend it until Easter. Certain brothers, like the Muslims, do not eat anything during the day but wait until the sun goes down to eat. Several abstain from eating to satiety; others eliminate from their meals ingredients that they prefer. By these privations, they create a solidarity with the Muslims while at the same time respecting their own Christian fast.

3.4 Pilgrimages

In Lebanon, in the Philippines and in Indonesia, the Franciscans and the Muslims get together each year to organize and experience a pilgrimage. Most often it consists of a walk for peace or for a social cause particularly during which Christians and Muslims walk, sing, fast, and pray God according to their own respective traditions. On occasion one sees Franciscans praying, chaplet in hand, and Muslims reciting on theirs, the ninety-nine names of Allah.

3.5 Interreligious Meetings

Some Islamic-Christian associations, coordinated by Franciscans, now exist in Italy, France, Belgium, Germany, Spain, Bosnia and Herzegovina, Indonesia, the Philippines, Singapore, Lebanon, Syria, Morocco, Canada, and the USA. These associations or centers have as their objective to encourage meetings, reflections, and collaborative efforts between Muslims and Christians. In Damascus, in Syria, the imam of the great mosque invited the Franciscans and the apostolic nuncio to their Friday prayer. Before an assembly of 6,000 people, he asked a Franciscan to comment on interreligious dialogue. The Franciscan recalled the event of the meeting between Francis of Assisi and the Sultan Malik al-Kamil in 1219,[54] and he invited Muslims and Christians to go beyond religious differences and seek together ways of collaborating in order to face the challenges of our societies and to help young people find their place in them. Since then, an Islamic-Christian association has opened a center to help "street-kids" to find work and to give them a place (library) to study.

On October 27, 1986, Assisi, the town of St. Francis, was the site of a gathering of the leaders of the principal religions in order to pray and fast for peace in the world. The 235 representatives of Christianity, Buddhism, Islam, Judaism, Jainism, Hinduism, Shintoism, Zoroastrism , as well as Sikhs and traditional African and native American religions, asked God's help and committed

---

[54] This meeting between the two men of different religions during the Crusades, had such an impact on Muslim-Christian relations that the Church continues to use it as motivation for inter-religious dialogue.

themselves to promote peace in the world. The effort undertaken since 1986 has stimulated initiatives of dialogue that have expressed themselves in different ways in different countries. Franciscans organize prayer meetings to which followers of several religions are summoned and in which Muslim officials take part. They are "together to pray" for peace in the world through prayers, chants, readings and silent meditation. These meetings have given birth to other events such as thematic religious exchanges: Isaac's sacrifice in monotheistic religions, the fundamentalist religious phenomenon, etc. These meetings increase ties and encourage the participants to go beyond their religious differences to create initiatives able to respond to the needs of all.

In certain countries such as Lebanon, Syria, and Egypt, Franciscans have initiated meetings of prayer and dialogue with Muslims (friends, imams, professors, students). These meetings aimed at first to be occasions of getting to know one another better through exchanges about beliefs, and the respective ways of living one's faith. With time these meetings have led to exchanges about social, religious, political, economic, and educational problems experienced there and in the world in order to seek answers and solutions together. For example, in neighborhoods of Bosnia and Herzegovina devastated by war, Franciscans and Muslims have built orphanages, schools, and dispensaries together. Even if the directors and the personnel of the institutions are Muslims and Franciscans, children are educated, cared for, and treated in consideration of each one's religious tradition. In a primary school situated in Tyr, Lebanon, means have been put into place by the Franciscans (directors of this institute) to respect the differences but also to avoid marginalizing one group to the detriment of the other or encouraging competition between the religions. (In activities in and outside school, the Muslims and Christians are not divided. Each class, each sports team, each social group includes youth from each religion. In a football match, for example, one does not see Muslims playing against Christians). The brothers also organize interreligious prayers where the young Muslims and Christians pray that the societies come to the aid of youth who suffer from isolation, injustice, alcoholism, drug addiction and the like.

In Basilan, in the Philippines, the Franciscans have built two Madrassas (schools) for teaching. The local fraternity produced a Yakan (local language) dictionary and a literacy text for adults. With the growing influences of fashion fads, young Muslims and Christians are adapting to the craze of the day to the detriment of their culture. Hence the friars revived Yakan weaving in order to safegaurd their cultural richness. Since then the jackets made with regional designs have become popular to the point where they are sold in large cities like Manila.

In Mindanao, still in the Philippines, the Franciscans invite Muslims and Christians to celebrate Christmas and they are invited to Muslim celebrations. They organize non-religious celebrations with the participation of Muslims and Christians. A lay person suggested the establishment of a Muslim-Christian office. Today this office is operational. It is directed alternately by a Muslim and a Christian. A dispensary where the care is based on traditional medicine is directed by a Muslim and a Franciscan.[55]

These initiatives, which aim to help the young and the less young to live in dignity, are born out of the parallels in the Franciscan and Muslim ways of prayer. Other initiatives can develop if we know how to take interest in and accept as valid prayers of other religions — initiatives lending hands to projects, achievements full of hope, initiatives which can come from Christians, Muslims, Jews, Buddhists, Hindus, Sikhs, from us, from you.

CONCLUSION

The true meeting ground between Muslim and Franciscan prayers and even among prayers of other religions is the attention to this "beyond" which alone justifies and founds them. Islam and Christianity, like other religions, have the same origin and the same ultimate end.[56] Believers are those who know that they come from

---

[55] Bertos, G., "Assalum... Towards the third millenium," *Among* 24 (IFCRM, 1995): 7-8.

[56] Nostra Aetate, *Vatican II*, Ed. Fides, Ottawa, 1967, p. 549.

somewhere else and that they will return there.[57] Prayer has this quality to transform this theoretical knowledge into practical knowledge and practice of existence. Prayer appears as one of the most fundamental places where religions may meet as long as the person believes in the strength of prayer. Even if the concept of prayer, like that of religion, is analogical, even if prayer has a different meaning according to the religion — and it is for this reason that we wanted to dwell not on its meaning, nor on its content, but rather on its form where parallels are most observable — it remains true to say that "prayer is a structure of religion."[58]

> *The act of prayer is a substantial movement of a person towards God...a point of support and a lever common to all religious spirits....there is no religion without prayer and there is no desire in faith without this desire leading to prayer....prayer is 'opening up to God.'*[59]

And if this be so, all respectful and welcome regard for the prayer of another must inevitably lead to a desire to come together to serve the well-being of humanity, to create links, to bring about new initiatives and inter-religious collaboration with a view to a better being and a better life together. These efforts will certainly contribute to going beyond the walls of difference.

BIBLIOGRAPHY

Abd-El-Jalil, J.–M. *Aspects intérieurs de l'Islam*. Paris: Éd. Seuil, 1950.
—, *L'Islam et nous*. Paris: Éd. Cerf, 1947.
Basetti-Sani, G., *Moḥammad et Saint-François*. Ottowa: Éd. Commissariat de Terre Sainte, 1959.

---

[57] J. Vidal, *L'Eglise et les Religions, ou le désir réorienté* (Paris: Albin Michel (Foi vivante), 1992) 72.
[58] Jean-Paul II, pp.71-72, 139, Vidal. op. cit.
[59] Monchanin, J., pp. 143-146 (cf. Vidal, p. 146).

Basset, J. C. *Le dialogue interreligieux. Histoire et avenir.* Cogitatio Fidei. Paris: Éd. Cerf, 1996.

Boespflug, F., et al., *Assise 10 ans après 1986-1996.* Paris: Éd. Cerf).

Boff, Leonardo. *François d'Assise.* Paris: Éd. Cerf, 1986.

Borrmans, M. *Jésus et les Musulmans d'aujourd'hui.* Jésus et Jésus Christ 69, Éd. Desclée, 1996.

—, *Orientations pour un dialogue entre chrétiens et musulmans.* Paris: Éd. Cerf, 1981.

Chebel, M. *Dictionnaire des symboles musulmans. Rite, mystique et civilisation.* Paris: Éd. Albin Michel, 1995.

—, *L'esprit d'oraison et de dévotion. Thème d'approfondissement et de réflexion.* Secrétariat général OFM pour la Formation et les Études. Rome: Curie générale des Frères Mineurs, 1996.

—, *Liturgie des Heures. Prière du temps présent.* Paris: *Cerf-Desclée-Desclée de Brouwer-Mame,* 1098; cf. Présentation de l'Office, XX-XL.

—, *Liturgy of the Hours.* New York: Catholic Book Publishing Co., 1975.

—, *Vatican II. Les seize documents conciliaires.* Texte intégral, 2è Ed. Fides. Montréal/Paris, 1967.

Corbin, H. *Histoire de la philosohie islamique, des origines à la mort d'Avérroès.* Paris, 1964.

Desbonnets, T. *De l'intuition à l'institution. Les Franciscains.* Paris: Éd. Franciscaines, 1983.

Desbonnets, T. et al., *Saint François d'Assise. Documents. Écrits et premières biographies.* 2e éd. Paris: Éd. Franciscaines, 1968.

De St-Renan, A. *Miettes Franciscaines.* Éd. N.-D. de la Trinité, Blois, 1961.

De Vitry, Meyerovitch. *Rûmî et le soufisme.* Coll. Maitres spirituels. Paris: Éd. Seuil, 1977.

Dubost, M. X. Lesort, S. Lalanne, V. Rouillard. *Théo., L'encyclopédie catholique pour tous.* Paris: Éd. Droguet, Ardant, Fayard, 1993.

Esser, K. *Origines et Objectifs primitifs de l'Ordre des Frères Mineurs.* Paris: Éd. Franciscaines, 1983; Leiden: Trad. de l'allemand par E.J. Brill, 1966.

Flood, D. *Frère François et le mouvement franciscain.* Éd. Ouvrières, Coll. Paris: Peuple de Dieu, 1983.

Habig, Marion et al., *St. Francis of Assisi. Writing and early biographies. English Omnibus of the Sources for the Life of St. Francis*, Ed. Marion A. Habig. Quincy, IL: Franciscan Press, 1972.

Hoeberichts, J. *Francis and Islam.* Quincy, IL: Franciscan Press, 1997.

Hubaut, M. *La voie franciscaine.* Paris: Éd.Desclée de Brouwer, 1983.

The Jerusalem Bible, Ed. Daron. London: Longman & Todd, 1960.

John–Paul II, *Cathéchisme de l'Église catholique.* Éd. Conférence des Évêques catholiques du Canada [CECC]. Ottowa, 1993.

Jeusset, G. *Rencontre sur l'autre rive, François d'Assise et les Musulmans.* Paris: Éd. Franciscaines, 1996.

Manselli, R. *Saint François d'Assise.* Paris: Éd Franciscaines, 1980.

Martimort, A.–G. et al. *L'Église en prière. Introduction à la liturgie.* 3e Ed. Paris: Desclée et Co., 1965.

Milot, J.–R. *L'islam et les musulmans.* Québec: Éd. Fides, 1993.

Paquette, F. et al., *Among.* Bulletin of the International Franciscan Commission for Relation with the Muslims [IFCRM]. Rome, 1993-1997.

—, *La prière dans l'islam.* En Bref. Montréal, 1996.

—, *L'islam et les frères mineurs.* Ed. International Franciscan Commission for Relation with the Muslims (IFCRM). Rome.

Schaluck, H. *Règle et Constitutions générales de l'Ordre des Frères Mineurs.* Paris: Éd. Franciscaines, 1991.

The Qur 'ān, *The Message of the Qur 'ān*, Translated and explained by Muhammad Asad. Gibraltar: Dar al-Andalus, 1980.

Vidal, J. *L'Eglise et les Religions, ou le désir réorienté.* Paris: Albin Michel [Foi vivante], 1992.

Vorreux, D. *Les écrits de saint François et de sainte Claire.* Paris: Éd. Franciscaines, 1988.

"I do no longer adore what you adore!"

The Exodus Motif
in Christianity and Islam

Its Relevance for the Dialogue
Between Islam and Franciscanism

Thomas Mooren, O.F.M. Cap.

He started for the door, then turned back. "Would Fletcher have made a good priest?" "No, Father," Tom answered without hesitation. "There's more to this job than memorizing scripture and church dogma." "What's he lacking?" The priest thought for a moment. "Compassion," he said softly.

Tami Hoag, Night Sins

1) Introduction

There are many possible avenues one can take while being in dialogue with the other, be it the other religion, the other political system, etc., or simply the other person as a human being. But whatever the approach we choose to take, we know that, once engaged towards the "otherness of the other," we have *to leave behind us* at least something of our own Self, i.e., of the old Self before we entered the road of dialogue. Everyone who has engaged into a true dialogue knows how a new Self may be born in the process — sometimes in a very painful way — a Self enriched by the presence of the other who knocks at my door and at whose door I knock.

Truly, this new, enriched Self is also one who has "lost weight" — illusions, prejudices, a couple of expectations and hopes and other similar things. However, if I had never left home, so to speak, I would not have learnt anything about the other-world out there, and consequently nothing about my own Self. I call this spiritual adventure during which, in one way or the other, we are leaving our Self behind us, the "exodus gesture." As we can easily see, the exodus gesture is essential for the dialogue. We have to summon the courage and energy of Abraham who once left his homeland, departing for a place only the Lord knows.[1]

But the exodus motif is not only of interest in pinning down the specific kind of mental awareness needed for a successful dialogue, that is, as a description of the mind-stage of the *participants* in any given dialogue process, but also opens up a road towards the understanding of the spirit of religion as such, of what a religion really means to its followers and to those who try to understand it. Particularly obvious is this in cases like Buddhism or Taoism and naturally in the case of the three great Semitic religions; Judaism, Christianity, and Islam, to name them in the order they have appeared in history.

Nobody for example can understand Buddhism without taking into account the story of Buddha leaving his home, for example, leaving behind himself his wife and his little son Rahula in order to strive for enlightenment. Here the touching story, certainly a crucial moment in Buddha's life:

> Now the Future Buddha... thought to himself, "I will take just one look at my son;" and, rising from the couch on which he was sitting, he went to the suite of apartments occupied by the mother of Rahula, and opened the door of her chamber. Within the chamber was burning a lamp fed with sweet-smelling oil, and the mother of Rahula lay sleeping on a couch strewn deep with jasmine and flowers, her hand resting on the head of her son. When the Future Buddha reached the threshold, he paused, and gazed at the two from where he stood.
>
> If I were to raise my wife's hand from off the child's head, and take him up, she would awake, and thus prevent my departure. "I will first become a Buddha, and then come back and see my son." So saying, he descended from the palace. (Warren 1978:62).

And who has not heard of Lao Tsu's *Tao Te King*, where the spirit of "exile," of breaking away from the world and going out into the

---

[1]For the dialogue process see also Mooren 1994:18-54, 107-114.

woods first and thereupon into one's own inner Self is omnipresent as the foundation of wisdom itself? Here are some words of chapter 64 of the famous book:

... He who acts defeats his own purpose;
He who grasps loses...
Therefore the sage seeks freedom from desire.
He does not collect precious things....
He brings men back to what they have lost.
He helps the ten thousand things find their own nature,
But refrains from action. (Feng and English 1972)

This certainly is a very highly interiorized form of exodus, but its sophisticated form of "inaction" does not mean laziness or "dolce vita." Rather it is the strength of the soft and the weak, the usefullness of what elsewhere is considered to be useless. Chapter 76 from the same book:

Thus an army without flexibility never wins a battle.
A tree that is unbending is easily broken.
The hard and strong will fall.
The soft and weak will overcome.

The purpose of these very brief hints to the exodus spirit in Buddhism and Taoism — not surprisingly two religions with strong "monastic" ties[2] — consists in showing us the spiritual potential of the exodus motif as something which is not limited to the three semitic-born religions but may serve as a topic with a far broader impact and aura.

The present paper, however, will concentrate on the exodus motif within Islam and Christianity which both inherited this topic from Judaism. The religious figure standing for it is Abraham.[3] And *in this sense* I think Abraham can serve as a link between Islam and Christianity. The impact of Abraham and with him the impact of the

---

[2]This is specially true for Buddhism. There we have a case where the foundation of a religious community (the sangha) coincides with the foundation of a new religion. Nevertheless the term *bhikkhu* ("almstaking") used for the member of the Buddhist order should not be translated by "monk", but by mendicant, friar or at least "wandermonk".

[3]Elsewhere (Mooren 1994:158/9, note 137) I laid down my reasons for the preference of the exodus of Abraham ordered to him by God in Gn, 12, 1 ("Go forth from the land of your kinsfolk and from your father's house!") as compared to the exodus via the Red Sea.

exodus motif on Christian theology, will be exemplified by the apostle Paul, while Abraham's and the exodus motif's importance for Muslim theology will be shown by studying the Holy Koran. The apostle Paul is chosen on the Christian side for three reasons. Firstly, he is the one who makes the most of Abraham in his theological effort to put Christian theology solidly on its own rails; secondly, he and not Jesus the Christ, is the one who should best be compared to the Prophet Moḥ ammad;[4] and thirdly, there is, in my opinion, no better Christian saint or theological writer to compare St. Francis with than St. Paul.

Thus, after having demonstrated through a comparison Paul — Muḥammad that the exodus motif is indeed part of the fabric of both the Christian and the Islamic theology, we will turn towards St. Francis studied specifically as the one who revived the exodus gesture in his time. And it is this aspect of his life and thought which, in my opinion, makes St. Francis the ideal figure for an ongoing dialogue between Muslims and Christians, particularly those Christians who take St. Francis as their spiritual guide and model.

2) The Exodus Motif and St. Paul

To ask for the role of the exodus gesture in the theology of St. Paul means that we have to look for the place Abraham takes in Paul's writings. This in turn leads us directly to Paul's epistle to the Galatians,[5] Clearly, here is not the place to enter into an exhaustive discussion of the complexity of Paul's message to the people of Galatia. It suffices for our purpose to remember that what is at stake in this letter is the problem of the *means* of salvation — salvation understood in terms of the classical biblical tradition — and the question, if the *Law* is still part of those means. Paul vigorously denies it. This is how Paul resumes his position: "Christ redeemed us from the curse of the Law by being cursed for our sake" (Gal 3, 13). In no way does the law function as means of salvation. It's role was only one of an interim player in the

---

[4]I for my part have come to this conclusion because of the many ambiguities which arise if one compares Jesus Christ — for Christians clearly a human person but *also* more than a human being, namely the "Son of God" and second person of the Trinity — with the Prophet Moḥammad who *never* claimed a *comparable* status for himself. See for this also Mooren 1996:68-70.

[5]For the following see Mooren 1996:70-79.

history of salvation, and even then it was not a happy one: thanks to the law the crimes increased (cf. Gal 3, 19).

The assessment of the law as being no longer useful for salvation is the result of Paul's personal experience of the risen Christ (1Cor 15, 8); in other words: the experience that the resurrection had overruled the eternal condemnation pronounced by the law about anyone dying on the cross (cf. Dt 21, 23; Gal 3, 13). Thus the road is opened up for a new player replacing the law: pistis, faith. And with faith Abraham enters the scene (Gal 3, 6): "Take Abraham for example: he put his faith in God...." Yet, this is not said because of a simple historical commemoration, or a pious rememberance of someone gone long ago, just in case you need a hero of the old ages in order to vigorize the mood of the people of the present time. Rather Abraham's faith is put forward because of the effect it had, the spiritual result it produced, namely justification: "... and this faith was considered as justifying him" (Gal 3, 6).

This, however, is important really only for one reason: faith is something which can be produced by a person without being a member of Israel according to the "flesh", faith has nothing to do with blood, and thus is accessible also to the non-Jews, the pagans! Faith is an existential gesture which can be put into motion by anybody at any time, while my kinship status is imposed upon me through birth. Thus, thanks to faith, a pagan can be justified and that means he/she can receive the *blessings* which go together with the justification, the blessings promised by God to Abraham (Gal 3, 8,9):

> Scripture forsaw that God was going to use faith to justify the pagans, and proclaimed the Good News long ago when Abraham was told: In you all pagans will be blessed. Those therefore who rely on faith receive the same blessing as Abraham, the man of faith.

In other words: the whole law-faith-justification-issue turns out to be really about this one single question: who is the child of Abraham and therefore heir of the promise made to him: "Don't you see that it is those who rely on faith who are the sons of Abraham?" (Gal 3, 7).

Obviously, and this has to be added, it is not faith hanging freely in the air. For Paul it is, naturally, faith in God (Gal 3, 6), but also faith in Christ (Gal 3, 22), since Christ was the one who, on the cross, severed the links between the Abraham's promise and a "Chosen People" on the basis of pure blood-relationship: "This was done so that in Jesus Christ the blessing of Abraham might include the pagans..." (Gal 3, 14).[6]

The only thing that Paul then still had to do in order to solidly anchor his Galatians into the ground of the "Promised Land" is to redefine, so to speak, the borders of this Land, i.e., its nature: "... so that in faith we might receive the promised Spirit" (Gal 3, 14). Thus the content of the promise is no longer children and territorial gain, but *pneuma*, the Spirit; more exactly that spirit in which, as Paul then explains, we can cry out: "Abba, Father!," while addressing God (Gal 4, 6,7). That is what it means to be Abraham's heir *now* (see Gal 3, 29). It means to be called to freedom (Gal 5, 13), the freedom of the children of God, and to a new creation (Gal 6, 15).

If we now ask about the exodus motif in this whole operation, we have to look at Abraham again, and to take into account the specific circumstances under which his faith was born. The epistle to the Galatians does not dwell on this point in an explicit manner, but every Abraham's son and daughter knew, when the whole faith story with Abraham began, namely with God's call in Gn 12, 1: "... leave your country, your family and your father's house, for the land I will show you." And Abraham "went as Yahweh told him...(he) was seventy-five years old when he left Haran" (Gen 12 4).[7]

But there is more to this. If we look, indeed, at Paul's program developed in enthusiastic words to his Galatian audience — a life no longer based upon the law (as exemplified by the circumcision fight; Gal, chap 5), a new creation based upon the Spirit and that means a life motivated by love ("...faith that makes its power felt through love," Gal 5, 6 etc) and sustained by the spirit of freedom (Gal 5, 13 – 15 etc.) — and if we also take into account who are the beneficiaries of this program, that is, the new heirs of Abraham — people of whatever origin or social condition, all equal because (and as long as) they are "clothed

---

[6]See also the argumentation of Gal 3, 16, where Abraham's posterity is *identified* with Christ.

[7]In his letter to the Romans Paul is more specific about the faith of Abraham. The whole fourth chapter of the letter dwells upon this point. It practically follows the theological outline of the letter to the Galatians, but insists more on the wonder of Abraham becoming father (and Sarah mother) inspite of old age as the point to belief and to have faith in. But this, in fact, is only an *additional* difficulty added to the faith problem. The first step, the very first concretization of Abraham's faith consisted in leaving the country, the exodus. The promise of having descendants is inseparably linked to this first step!

in Christ,"[8] — we have to acknowledge that *Paul's Gospel itself* (Gal 1, 2, 11, 12) is a real exodous action. His Gospel is a true *break-away* from the old type of Chosen People,[9] and it is an action at least as daring (if not even more so) as Abraham's exodus towards new shores.

How daring Paul's action is becomes clear, if we realize that in breaking away from the standards of the old Chosen People Paul, in his attempt to found a New Chosen People (the new creation, the New People of God) through the reiteration, in his own way, of Abraham's faith-gesture, not only rivals this most venerated patriarch, but with the great Moses himself, the founder of the first Chosen People.[10]

To go back so far in the history of salvation is certainly not too bold for a man who calls himself an apostle "who does not owe his authority to men or his appointment to any human being but who has been appointed by Jesus Christ and by God the Father who raised Jesus from the dead" (Gal 1, 1).[11] And as the authority comes directly from God so does the message : "...the Good News I preached is not a human message that I was given by men, it is something I learnt only through a revelation of Jesus Christ" (Gal 1, 12).

In fact this does make Paul not only a "dissident" — if we may use this term here in a very broad sense[12] — from Old Israel, but puts him also into a rather awkward position in front of his new companions and allies, the Christians, as the whole circumcision story (Gal, 2) reveals —

---

[8]"All baptized in Christ, you have all clothed yourselves in Christ, and there are no more distinctions between Jew and Greek, slave and free, male and female, but all of you are one in Christ Jesus" (Gal 3, 28).

[9]This does not exclude that later, in the letter to the Romans, Paul passionately argues for the inclusion, under condition, of the old Chosen People into the new one, namely in his famous simile of the shoots of wild olive. There Paul talks, for example, about the possibility that the Jews "if their give up their unbelief', may be "grafted back" (Rm 11, 23) on the olive tree. He even acknowledges in Rm 4, 12 that Abraham can function as ancestor not only of the pagans, but also "of those who though circumcised do not rely on that fact alone, but follow our ancestor Abraham along the path of faith he trod before he had been circumcised." However, Paul's concern for "Old Israel" does not invalidate my argument concerning his break-away-action. For the question of the development of Paul's thinking, see the discussion in Mooren 1991:345-347.

[10]We could also say that Paul rivals with Moses via Abraham. For Paul as a "second Moses" see also Taubes 1993:57.

[11]Again Gal 1, 15: "Then God, who had specially chosen me while I was still in my mother's womb...."

[12]See for this example Owomoyela 1991:21-48, where use and misuse of the term "dissidence," particularly if taken out of its original context (the human right struggle in the communist countries of Eastern Europe) is discussed in some length.

so much so that Paul "opposed (Peter) to his face" in this matter (Gal 2, 11). Broadening up the newly emerged Christian community, through the elimination of the Jewish Law as means of salvation, to the pagan peoples, is perhaps an even greater exodus from the old trodden path of salvation than Paul's first exodus-gesture when he turned away from persecuting Christians (Gal 1, 13) since he had found the risen Christ before Damascus (Acts 9, 1 - 19).

For Paul, however, theses two exodus gestures, the conversion and the vocation to be the apostle of the gentiles, have merged into one. In Gal 1, 16 he mentions them in a single breath. This certainly makes sense, since both, conversion and mission, are rooted in the same event: the crucifixion. The cross defeats the law as means of salvation, as we have seen above (cf. Gal 3, 13), the cross opens the road to the nations and thus to the universalization of the Abraham blessings (Gal 3, 14). Therefore, when Paul states that God "called me... to reveal his son in me..." (Gal 1, 16), it really means that Paul has to reveal the "mystery of the cross" which is the true summit of his (and any Christian's) exodus experience since the cross is the true and most radical *reversal* of the values of the "world",[13] of what the "world" thinks to be wisdom:

> The language of the cross may be illogical... to the Jews (it is) an obstacle that they cannot get over, to the pagans madness, but to those who have been called, whether they are Jews or Greeks (we preach a crucified Christ) who is the power and the wisdom of God. For God's foolishness is wiser than human wisdom, and God's weakness is stronger than human strength (1Cor 1, 18, 23 – 25).

It is his faithfulness to the "illogical language" of the cross which makes Paul, certainly one of the most singled out persons in the history of religions, a true servant of Christ (Gal 1, 10). The cross, and that always includes the resurrection, is the root for Paul's boldness described above, the motor, so to speak, of his life-long exodus adventure.

---

[13]Cf. Mooren 1996:75/6; Taubes 1993:37/8.

3)   The Exodus Motif and the Prophet Muḥammad

If we now turn to the Prophet Muḥammad in our investigation we
have to keep in mind the purpose of this chapter as I have outlined it in
the introduction. Accordingly my intention in the following lines is not
to discuss what the cross and the death of Jesus, the status of Jesus as
Son of God, the concept of salvation and the role of the law etc. have
become in Islamic theology as compared to Christian doctrine.
Everybody knows how far away the official positions of Islam and
Christianity are on these matters and many others.[14] Rather shall I
concentrate, in a more *formal* or structural approach, on the following
questions: what is the role of Abraham in the theology of the Prophet?
Or more exactly: does the Prophet Muḥammad use the patriarch in a
way similar to Paul so that Abraham will lead us, as he did in the case of
Paul, to the *exodus* motif? Is the Prophet Muḥammad too, in his own
way, a second Abraham, and, as I said with regard to Paul, a kind of
religious dissident? If so, i.e., if the exodus motif is indeed part of the
fabric of Islamic theology and of being a true Muslim, we then could at
least acknowledge a cultural-psychological brotherhood between these
two great Semites, St. Paul and the Prophet Muḥammad — and that
would not be the smallest merit of the approach proposed in the present
chapter!

Any attempt to answer the above posed questions[15] has to begin
with a reminder of the core message of Islam, namely the absolute
indivisible unity of God (tahuid) as it is expressed, for example, in sūra
112:[16]

> Say: He, God, is One.
> God is He on Whom all depend.
> He begets not, nor is He begotten.
> And none is like Him.

This message, however, in the eyes of the Prophet Muḥammad is
not a new one. Other Prophets before him had already been called to

---

[14]Cf. too Talbi 1972:49.

[15]For the following see also Mooren 1996:79-93.

[16]All the translations of the Holy Qur`ān, if not otherwise indicated, follow *The
Qur`ān*, transl. by Shakir, with the exception of the term "Allāh" which I render by
"God", and the term "ḥanīf" which I keep untranslated.

preach it (cf. sūra 2, 136, 285; 4, 163/4 etc.).[17] What is new, are the historical circumstances under which the Prophet Muḥammad has to accomplish his work. These circumstances are charcterized by a double challenge emanating from both groups the Jews and the Christians. The challenge consists in the claim that the time of revelation is over, that the books are closed. For the Christians they are closed in Christ and the Church, for the Jews in the Promised Land and the Torah. And even if the Jews are still waiting for a Messiah, it is clear that he has to come within the lines of the covenant which runs through Isaac and not Ismail or anybody else.[18]

The Holy Qur'ān has a name for this kind of conviction held up by Jews and Christians. It is called: the tying up of God's hand:

> And the Jews say: The hand of God is tied up! Their hands shall be shackled and they shall be cursed for what they say. Nay, both His hands are spread out, He expends as He pleases... (sūra 5, 64).

The Prophet in particular takes issue with the privileges both Jews and Christians think they can draw from this situation:

> And the Jews and Christians say: We are the sons of God and His beloved ones... (sūra 5, 18).

And therefore:

> ... they say: None shall enter the... paradise... except he who is a Jew or a Christian. These are their vain desires. Say: bring your proof if you are truthful (sūra 2, 111).

In other words, what Muḥammad's opponents claim is nothing less than a *monopoly* in matters of revelation,[19] a monopoly from which they then draw exclusive rights over the *blessings* which go with it. Thus the task for the Prophet is clear. He has to break up this claim in order to create space for his own message and for the community of his followers. He will, on this road, eventually end up as the seal, i.e., the

---

[17]Cf. Fontaine 1972:25/6.

[18]Paul echoes this conviction in Gal 4, 21 - 31

[19]Compared to the claim of the Jews and the Christians, the religion of the pagan Arabs is, theologically speaking, a minor threat for the message of the Prophet. See for this too Mooren 1996:91/2 (note 244), and ibid., 113 (note 298).

perfection of prophecy (sūra 33, 40) and be surrounded by a community (umma) which is the best thinkable on earth (sūra 3, 110). The question then for us is, how did he get there? What was, so to speak, the lever he could use in the arena of theological arguments, in order to make his position heard?[20] The answer to these questions holds in one word: Abraham! He is the lever. He opens the road.

There is, however, a problem. As much as Paul, in order to build up his version of the People of God, had to "baptize" or christianize Abraham since this is the name the theological operation we have studied in chapter two really merits,[21] so does the Prophet Muḥammad have to *islamize* the famous patriarch. Or maybe we should put this into a slightly different way: the islamization of Abraham is not a problem, rather it is the whole point the Prophet can make while trying to break up the claims of his predecessors in salvation history. How does he do it? He proceeds in three steps.[22] He first *deconfessionalizes* Abraham:

> Nay! do you say that Ibrahim and Ismail and Yaqoub... were Jews or Christians? Say: Are you better knowing or God? (sūra 2, 140).

Or sūra 3, 67:

> Ibrahim was not a Jew nor a Christian...

But who was he then? He simply was the first *Muslim!*[23] Having been liberated from the exclusive ideological grasp by Jews and Christians, he can now be seen as the one he really was. Here the continuation of sūra 3, 67:

> ...but he was...a Muslim, and he was not one of the polytheists.

The same, i. e. that Abraham or his posterity were Muslims, is also said in sūra 2, 128 (two times), 131, 132, 133, 136; 3, 84; 4, 125; 22, 34,

---

[20]In other words: this is how I try to show the relevance of the exodus motif for Islamic theology, namely by analyzing *some* aspects of the Prophet's message in the wake of the Jewish and Christian claim to soteriological exclusiveness. Nowhere is a *general* theological survey of the Islamic message intended.

[21]Throughout the letter to the Galatians Paul, indeed, acts according to his claim that Christ is Abraham's *only posterity* (Gal 3, 16).

[22]Obviously these are logical steps. No historical order is intended.

[23]The term "Muslim" here is obviously not used in the later strict confessional/denominational sense as the following shows.

78; 37, 103. Giving Abraham this decisive name, claiming him to be one of his (Muḥammad's) group as a Muslim "avant la lettre", so to speak,[24] and thus indirectly presenting himself as a second Abraham, is the second step in the Prophet's strategy to get in line with "salvation history", i.e., with the promise made by God to Abraham, and to face his opponents' claims.[25]

After having deconfessionalized Abraham, an operation which in turn opened the road to formally bestowing a *new* confession, namely muslimhood upon the patriarch,[26] the third step of the Prophet's strategy to put forward his own soteriological claim consists in consolidating the link between Abraham and the time of the Prophet, i. e., the historical community of Muslims. In order to achieve this goal the Holy Qur `ān establishes a *genealogical* relationship between the patriarch and the Arabs, namely the Meccans, and declares him and his son Ismail the founders of the Ka'ba, the principal sanctuary of Islam. (See sūra 2, 124 - 129; 14, 35, 37, 39, 40).[27]

Thus the Prophet has broken up the claim to exclusivity voiced by his predecessors in salvation history. He has put himself solidly in line with Abraham and thus made sure that his community of the faithful is theologically legitimized. It is above all this kind of *theological* blessing the Prophet inherits from Abraham, the real teacher of Islam itself.[28] To

---

[24]That is, before the appearance of the historical, official Islām.

[25]He even does better, so to speak, than Paul in the epistle to the Galatians, since, once having claimed Abraham and his posterity for his cause, the Holy Qur `ān bestows muslimhood, or an invitation to it, upon a whole series of venerable people in the Old Testament, like Noah (sūra 10, 72), Joseph (sūra 7, 126) etc. For details see Lüling 1981:252. Obviously, we have to take the term "muslim" here in the double sense of "true believer in the One God" at any given time *and* follower of the *Prophet's* cause.

[26]As already explained, "muslimhood" is new only because of the historical circumstances. In reality it is the "old" authentic Abraham confession.

[27]See Abraham's prayer in sūra 2, 128, after having built the Ka'ba with Ismail (sūra 2, 125): "Our Lord, make Ismail and me Muslims and (form) from our offspring a community (umma) of Muslims!" (my translation) And sūra 2, 129 clearly forsees the Prophet Muhammad emerging from Abraham's offspring: "O Lord! And raise up in them an Apostle from among them who shall recite to them Thy communications and teach them the Book and the wisdom, and purify them...." Obviously, the genealogical argument is purely ideological in nature and does not depend on a somatic verification. Furthermore it must be added that genealogical ties alone are by no means a warranty for salvation: "My covenant does not include the unjust, said He (God)" (sūra 2, 124). See too Mooren 1981b:555.

[28]See sūra 2, 125, and Abraham's prayer to God in 2, 128: "... and show us our ways of devotion...".

be sure, part of the blessing is also the transformation of Mecca into a "sure town" providing "its people with fruits" (see sūra 2, 126). But that does not outwit the theological gain, to have broken up the claim of the Jews and the Christians to be the only ones worthy to enter paradise.

However, to break up the claim to exclusivity defended by the Jews and Christians also means to break away from them. Thus the Prophet formally accomplishes a true exodus gesture[29] which, as such, in the eyes of Jews and Christians can only be considered as a defiant gesture of *"dissidence"* on Muḥammad's part.[30]

This, however, would not have come as a surprise to the Prophet. He clearly was aware of the dissident aspect, so to speak, of his faith gesture, since it exactly indicated the circumstances under which the faith of his spiritual father Abraham had come into being. When Abraham embraced true monotheism, i.e., when he became a Muslim "avant la lettre", he did so in defiance of his own people. He even had to break with his own father! Sūra 60, 4:

> Indeed, there is for you a good example in Ibrahim and those with him when they said to their people: Surely we are clear of you and of what you serve besides God; we declare ourselves to be clear of you, and enmity and hatred have appeared between us and you forever until you believe in God alone....

It is only with regard to his own "non-muslim" father that Abraham hopes to be able to build a "bridge of forgiveness": "I would certainly ask forgiveness for you" (sūra 6, 40). And he does so in sūra 26, 86: "And forgive my father, for surely he is of those who have gone astray". But Abraham knows that he does not control the heart of his father, nor the mysterious ways of God (sūra 6, 40: "I do not control for you aught from God"), and does not really seem to believe that his prayer would do any good. He prayed for his father, but only because he had promised him to do so (sūra 19, 47). In the end Abraham had no choice but to give his father up, to break away from him. That must have been

---

[29]Particularly if we consider the possibility that the Prophet himself was no stranger to Mecca's judeo-christian milieu. See for this Mooren 1996:84, note 222, and ibid., 91/2, note 244.

[30]We have, however, to mention here that Mohammad's theological operation can also be understood, on the part of the Christians, as the fulfillment of the promise made to *Ismail (Ishmael)* in Gn 16, 10/11; 17, 20; 21, 18. See for this Hayek 1964 and 1972; Mooren 1981a:53-72 and 1991:41-52.

a great pain for him, the good Semitic son, but the result is there:

> And Ibrahim asking forgiveness for his sire was only owing to a promise which he had made to him; but when it became clear to him that he was an enemy of God, he declared himself to be clear of him... (sūra 9, 114).[31]

Seen from a Semitic standpoint, Abraham's "I do no longer adore what you adore!" could not have taken a more radical shape than this breaking up of the closest family ties. It really makes the patriarch merit a title which is practically of equal importance as his being called a Muslim, namely ḥanīf. The already quoted sūra 3, 67 calls him such in the same breath with the term Muslim. We certainly can expect that one explains the other, so much "ḥanīf" seems to be Abraham's religion:

> Surely Ibrahim was an exemplar, obedient to God, a ḥanīf, and he was not of the polytheists... Follow the faith of Ibrahim, the ḥanīf... (sūra 16, 120, 123).

And in sūra 6, 161 the Prophet confesses:

> ... Surely, (as for) me, my Lord has guided me to the right path;
>
> (to) a most right religion, the faith of Ibrahim, a ḥanīf....

The same direction is taken by sūra 4, 125:

> And who has a better religion than he who submits himself entirely to God? And he is the doer of good (to others) and follows the faith of Ibrahim, the ḥanīf, and God took Ibrahim as a friend. (See too sūra 2, 130, 135; 3, 65, 68, 95).

There is no doubt, a ḥanīf in the Holy Qur 'ān is an extremely positive figure, characterized by submission to God, obedience, living as God's friend.[32] Seen from this angle a ḥanīf is indeed a good Muslim. However, the term ḥanīf can signify all this only after having gone through the most spectacular surgery on the level of meaning, since it

---

[31]The sūra ends, however, with an astonishing declaration: "Ibrahim was very tenderhearted, forbearing."(!) For Abraham and his father, see too Mooren 1996:82/3.

[32]See too sūra 30, 30: "Set your face upright for the (only true) religion. (Do so) as a ḥanīf. It is the religion of the very first day of creation (ḥanīf — fiṭra) handed over to the human beings. There is no altering of God's creation. That is the right religion, but most people do not know..." (my translation). In other words, in the end we assist at the equation between Islam, Abraham and the very first and therefore the very best religion which has ever existed on earth — and all this in the name of ḥanīfism.

really means someone who has turned his back on something/someone, who has broken up a relationship, being full of contempt for what he/she leaves behind — in sum, it would not be inappropriate to translate ḥanīf by "dissident" or heretic.[33]

Yet, this can be put also in another way, since the matter really depends on what or whom you turn your back, with whom you break up, what or whom you leave behind. In other words: since there is nothing wrong in leaving the devil behind, it finally depends on *who* defines orthodoxy. In our case the term ḥanīf turns positive, because the Prophet himself, being convinced to follow Abraham's example, assumed it wholeheartedly. He thus changes what his predecessors in salvation history could only call a heresy into the purest form of orthodoxy. In his eyes his breaking away, his exodus gesture is a positive, i. e. justified one, since he leaves behind theological falsehood: the gates of paradise being closed for non-Jews and non-Christians, the polytheism of the pagans, and its more subtle version of multiplying Gods via trinity and mariology.[34]

But this is not all. The very same dynamics which are at work concerning the term ḥanīf are at work again with regard to the core term "Islām" itself, since "Islām" and "Muslim" too, both derived fom the verbal form *aslama* offer the meaning: "to forsake, leave, desert, give up, betray" (Wehr 1974:425). It is the *redefinition* of orthodoxy by the Prophet Muḥammad which turns "Islām" into "submission, resignaton, reconciliation (to the will of God)" (Wehr 1974:426).[35]

Islam as submission *begins* with Abraham's "I do no longer adore what you adore!," strongly echoed by the Prophet himself in sūra 109, 2, 4 - 6: "...I do not adore what you adore..., nor am I going to do so. Nor

---

[33]Thus the idea, voiced by some specialists, that a ḥanīf was a non-orthodox monk, an ascetic who had left the main churches in order to adore the One God beyond the dogmatic quarrels of the theologians (cf. Rodinson 1961:89/90). However, the important thing for us is not that those ascetics may have been called by this term, but that Abraham, i.e., the Muslims themselves stick to it. The negative image of ḥanīf is also fueled by what the term means in the Semitic sisterlanguages, where it goes from pagan, atheistic (Syriac), to pervers (Hebrew), arrogant and of false mind (Aramaic), or without piety (Ugaritic). See too Hayek 1959:136-152; Moubarac 1958:151-161; Mooren 1991:44, note 42.

[34]Sūra 5, 116/7: "And when God will say: O Isa son of Marium! did you say to men, Take me and my mother for two gods besides God... I (Isa) did not say to them aught save what Thou didst enjoin me with...".

[35]See too Mooren 1996:84/5..

are you going to adore Him whom I adore. You shall have your religion and I shall have mine"[36] — i.e., by an action of defiance, even if this leads the Prophet into exile[37] and never ending hardship. But what are adversities of all kind if compared to the strength of faith, a faith which is convinced to follow Abraham, ḥanīf and Muslim!

I think it has become clear by now that there are similarities in the lives of Paul and Muḥammad and that it is indeed possible to organize the "family ressemblance" between these two great Semites with the help of the exodus motif. We are dealing with similarities concerning the *formal gesture* of faith, i.e., both, Paul and Muḥammad *break away* from older structures towards new shores in the name of Abraham, the archetypical biblical "dissident," so to speak, both trying to make sure that their communities are solidly in line with him since he is the one with whom the *blessings* start or rather, after Adam and Noah, restart.

In other words, what I want to show is not, who has the truth, Paul or Muḥammad, but *how* both are running for it. But if there has to be a competition between these two truth seekers and their communities we should not forget the most important competition of all — inspite of all legitimate questioning on the dogmatic-theological level —, namely the one in matters of "good deeds" as pointed out by sūra 5, 48: "... therefore strive with one another to hasten to virtuous deeds; to God is your return, of all (of you), so He will let you know that in which you differed."

If there is one who has ever taken up this challenge by insisting that love and compassion, i.e., the essence of "virtuous deeds," always accompany "theological correctness" — it is St. Francis of Assisi, the subject of our last chapter.

4) The Exodus Motif and St. Francis

The first thing which comes to mind in the light of the statement made at the end of the previous chapter is St. Francis' revolutionary approach to mission work. His new vision about how to be a missionary is expressed in the chapter 16 of the rule of 1221. Here the mission work unfolds into two methods. While the classical way consists in "calling on

---

[36]My translation.

[37]The Hijra sept. 622 to Yathrib/Medina

(the) hearers to believe in God almighty, Father, Son, and Holy Spirit," but, and this is typical for St. Francis, only when the missionaries "see that (this kind of open proclamation) is God's will," St. Francis introduces also another way of being witness to Christ: "One way is to avoid quarrels or disputes and be subject to every human creature for God's sake" according to 1 Pet. 2, 13.[38]

The respect for the other which is shown by this passage as much as the spirit of humility and service are features which occur over an over again in the writings of St. Francis and his biographers.[39] Yet, there is nothing surprising about it, since this kind of humble service is the brand-name of St. Francis and his followers:

> No one is to be called "Prior". They are all to be known as "Friars Minor" without distinction, and they should be prepared to wash one another's feet.[40]

However, the important thing to understand in this matter with regard to our present investigation is the following: behind the Franciscan love and compassion, i.e., behind its *minoritas*, we can find the exodus motif as the foundation of such a spiritual attitude. St. Francis is humble, helpful, understanding, compassionate, etc., *because* he has undergone a most radical internal as much as external exodus: he has *left behind* his Ego, desire, glory and money, home, and family for the service of the Lord.

The first chapter of the Rule of 1221 clearly bears witness to this. It accumulates verbs which describe the action of breaking away, or leaving behind: following Christ's footsteps, selling one's belongings, coming after Christ, self-denial, taking up the cross, hating father and mother, leaving house and family etc.[41] Like a true leitmotif this one great topic is, so to speak, hammered into the hearts and minds of St. Francis' followers. Here the sounds of the spiritual swing, the heartbeat

---

[38]All quotations from the rule are taken from *St. Francis of Assisi, Omnibus of Sources*, here abbreviated: *Omnibus*.

[39]In the same spirit chapter 5 of the same rule of 1221 f. ex. insists on instructing and correcting sinful brothers "with humble charity" as true *servants* according to Mt. 28, 26 - 28 (*Omnibus*, 36) and so on.

[40]Chapter 6 of the rule of 1221, *Omnibus*, 37. Cf. too Celano's *First Life*, chapter 15, *Omnibus*, 260.

[41]The same is true for the story in St. Bonaventure's *Major Life*, chapter 3, which relates how St. Francis found the rule for his life (*Omnibus*, 647-8).

of the whole rule, of St. Francis' whole life can be perceived. Here the switch is thrown for the course to run. From here on, as the rule continues in chapter 2 (cf. *Omnibus*, 31), there is no "looking back" allowed any more.[42]

Most dramatically the exodus motif is shaped in the story relating how St. Francis broke up with his father, leaving behind a father on earth in exchange for a father in heaven: "Until now I called you my Father, but from now on I can say without reserve, 'Our father who art in heaven'" (Bonaventure, *Major Life*, *Omnibus*, 643). The result is total *freedom* for the service of the Lord, even if this transforms St. Francis momentarily into a kind of *civil "dissident:"*

> When the authorities saw how enraged (St. Francis' father) was, they sent a messenger to summon Francis. But he answered that, since by divine grace he had obtained freedom he was the servant of God and therefore no longer owed obedience to the civil authorities...."[43]

Again, it is disobedience *for the Lord's sake*: "And so the servant of the most high King was left stripped of all that belonged to him, that he might follow the Lord whom he loved,"[44] or as Celano's *Second Life* has it: "O generous spirit, to whom Christ alone is sufficient!" (*Omnibus*, 372). Also the rule of 1221 states most forcefully: "No matter where they are, the friars must always remember that they have themselves given up completely and handed over their whole selves to our Lord Jesus Christ...."[45]

It is this Christ-centered kind of freedom[46] which is the nerve of St. Francis' spiritual and material *poverty*. His "genuine love for poverty," as St. Bonaventure in his *Major Life* (*Omnibus*, 642) puts it,[47] makes possible St. Francis' freedom, (for example in his dealings with his

---

[42]See too: "Nothing then, must keep us back, nothing separate us from (God), nothing come between us and him" (Chapter 23 of the Rule of 1221, *Omnibus*, 52).

[43]*Legend of the three Companions*, *Omnibus*, 908.

[44]St. Bonaventure, Major Life, *Omnibus*, 643.

[45]Chapter 16, *Omnibus*, 44.

[46]See again St. Bonaventure's *Major Life*: "(St. Francis) was armed with the cross, the means of salvation which would enable him to escape from the shipwrecked world" (*Omnibus*, 643).

[47]See too the same author's Minor Life, chapter 3, *Omnibus*, 807-8: "For poverty's sake (St. Francis) left his father and mother and abandoned everything he had. No one was so greedy for gold as he was for poverty; no one ever guarded a treasure more carefully than he guarded this Gospel pearl."

father), while both, freedom and poverty, are only the other side of a life conceived as a permanent exodus in Christ's name: "We have left everything behind us; we must be very careful now not to lose the kingdom of heaven for so little" as money,[48] or: "...meanwhile free yourself from all that may hinder you, so that when the grace of Christ comes to you, He may find you well disposed in faith and devotion."[49] This same exodus spirit makes St. Francis leave behind "the men of long ago," while others, even well-intentioned religious superiors may cling to them.[50]

In sum, the change in perspective produced by the exodus spirit is so radical that, what was called "home" before, is now called "exile" — a life in the loving presence of God being from now on the only criterion of what home is and what not.[51] Given this reversal of values it should not cause wonder that even the destination of natural life is transformed, so that the day of St. Francis' death changes itself into "the day of his true birth."[52]

After these short and by no means exhaustive reflections on the life and the message of St. Francis,[53] which clearly show him as a man of the exodus, it does not come as a surprise at all that St. Francis, *under this specific aspect*, falls perfectly well in line with the two other exodus figures discussed in the present paper, St. Paul and the Prophet Muḥammad.

Thus, the similarity between Francis and Paul, to begin with, is so obvious, particularly in the light of the exodus motif, that we can almost qualify the life and the teaching of St. Francis a layout or a remake of Paul's christological adventure. St Francis, a convert in his own kind, i.e., from within as St. Paul was one from the "outside," is a living example of the foolishness of the cross preached and experienced by Paul, that is an example of the reversal of all "sound" earthen values for Christ's sake.

---

[48]Chapter 8 of the rule of 1221, *Omnibus*, 38. See too chapter 22 of the same rule, *Omnibus*, 47-50; the admonition about *Religious Life in Hermitages*: "The first care should be to seek the kingdom of God and his justice" (*Omnibus*, 72) etc.

[49]*Little Flowers of St. Francis*, *Omnibus*, 1355. See too Celano's *First Life*: "... (St. Francis) renounced the world and gave himself to Christ" (*Omnibus*, 322-3).

[50]*Mirror of Perfection*, *Omnibus*, 1166.

[51]Cf. St. Bonaventure's *Minor Life*, chapter IV, *Omnibus*, 811.

[52]*Mirror of Perfection*, *Omnibus*, 1251. See to Celano's description of St. Francis' death in the sign of the Passover (*First Life*, *Omnibus*, 323/3).

[53]These reflections, by the way, have been spiritual in nature. They have deliberately left aside the historical-exegetical dimension of the texts.

Furthermore, in both cases the texts portray the paradox of a human being of extreme humility, but nevertheless driven by an equally solid "spiritual pride," because they do not owe anything to anybody, except the divine Spirit itself.[54] Both are also, in their own way, and *as the result* of their exodus gesture, founders of a New People of God. We have studied this aspect of Paul's activity in chapter 2. Here a testimony about the *friars* as God's "new people":

> One day blessed Francis said to the brothers: "The Order of Friars Minor is a little flock that the Son of God in these latter times has asked of his Father, saying to him: 'Father, it is my wish that you rise up and give to me a new and humble people who, in this hour, will distinguish themselves by their humility and poverty from all those who have preceded them and who will be content to possess me alone as their sole riches.' And the Father said to his well-beloved Son: 'My son, your request is fulfilled'...."[55]

Being a "people" founded from within — the text just quoted is obviously colored by eschatological fervor proper to certain spiritual groups of the Franciscan movement — the friars are not adding any new *salvific* elements to the Church, except the evangelic striving for perfection,[56] a specific kind of *intensity* to live the Christian life.[57] And since they are supposed to strive harder, also their blessings are abundant, even if they can be resumed in *one* word alone: Christ![58] But

---

[54]See the numerous "God inspired me" and the famous "God gave me some friars", and "the Most High himself made it clear to me" etc. in St. Francis' *Testament* (*Omnibus*, 67-8), while St. Bonaventure talks about "God's secret revelations" heard by St. Francis (*Major Life, Omnibus*, 643). See also ibid., 646 etc.

[55]*Legend of Perugia, Omnibus*, 1043.

[56]"If you wilt be perfect go, sell..., and give" etc. (Rule of 1221, *Omnibus*, 31). See too *Legend of the Three Companions*: "Either these men are following the Lord in great perfection, or they must be demented, since their way of life appears desperate, with little food and going about barefoot and clad in the poorest garments" (*Omnibus*, 922).

[57]Therefore St. Francis' serious attempt to put into practice Gal 3, 28 the equality of all Christians in Christ bound only by the single command of love (Gal 5, 14) as can be seen in chapter 6 of the rule of 1221, *Omnibus*, 37.

[58]Those who live the gospel according to the rule receive a hundred-fold and eternal life, and will enter in possession of the kingdom — see Rule of 1221, chapter 1, quoting Mt 19, 29 and chapter 23, quoting Mt 25, 34 (*Omnibus*, 32, 5). See too the *Legend of the Three Companions, Omnibus*, 921: "Let us beware that, having left all things, we do not forfeit eternal life...." But eternal life, kingdom or the hundred-fold come really down only to one thing, or better person: Christ. See again the *Legend of Perugia*: "...to possess me alone as their sole riches" (*Omnibus*, 1043).

again, in all this St. Francis and his friars fit perfectly well into the picture drawn already by St. Paul before them: the exodus, the new people, the blessings.

Yet, Francis differs from Paul in this: he does not use any explicit theological reference to Abraham. There is, however, no specific need for him to do so, since he is already through baptism a well-established heir of the divine promise made to this patriarch. And yet — what is more Abraham-like than Francis' battle with his father — the Abraham of the Holy Qur`ān that is? Where else in the Christian world has there been such a meaning-laden dramatic illustration of the Qur`ānic "I do not adore what you adore"?

And that is not all. As much as St. Francis was convinced that God had directly instructed him,[59] so was the Prophet Muḥammad (see sūra 53, 1 - 18 etc.). In the same line we can also point out to St. Francis' deep understanding of another key term of Qur`ānic Spirituality, namely the *will* of God which was for Francis as much a fact of life[60] as it was for the Prophet Muḥammad. Thus, it was their perception of what God's will is, which led both of them, the Prophet and St. Francis, to the foundation of a new people of God, here the *umma*, there the order of the Friars Minor.

Finally I like to draw attention to the really ḥanīf-like treatment of *poverty* by St. Francis. Maybe nowhere the affinity between the Prophet and St. Francis on the phenomenological level[61] runs deeper than in this matter. We have seen above in chapter three that Qur`ānic ḥanīfism basically consists in turning what could be thought of in negative terms into something positive, into a spiritual and doctrinal gain! The same thing is true for St. Francis with regard to poverty. No one ever turned the despised and miserable lifestyle of a beggar and alms receiver into a *forma vitae* of highest virtue as Francis did, so much so that begging and alms are the true blessings for the friar. They are their authentic heritage — as if, so to speak, *poverty* was the promise made to Abraham and not richness and power! And it is no one else than Christ himself who pushes Francis into this kind of reversal, i.e., his ḥanīfism in

---

[59]See above, note 53.

[60]See the rule of 1221, chapter 16, with regard to the open proclamation of the gospel (*Omnibus*, 43) etc.

[61]This level does not imply identity of *motives* for action, but concentrates on formal or structural similarities.

matters of poverty:

> Alms are an inheritance and a right which is due to the poor because our Lord Jesus Christ acquired this inheritance for us.[62] (Rule of 1221, chapter 9, *Omnibus*, 39).

And in the *Mirror of Perfection* we read:

> My dearest brothers,... do not be ashamed to go out for alms, for our Lord made Himself poor in this world for our sakes... This is our heritage, which our Lord Jesus Christ has won and bequeathed to us...."[63] (Chapter 18, *Omnibus*, 1143).

Yet, this ḥanīfism in matters of poverty is backed by the even greater reversal operated in the name of *minoritas* in general: "We Friars Minor, servants and worthless as we are..."[64] — for example, the true spirit of love and compassion!

I think we have now gathered enough elements to substantiate the claim that the exodus motif does indeed fulfill a bridge-building function between Islam and Christianity and in particular between Islam and Franciscanism. Not only is the exodus spirit, as it is the case in all true forms of dialogue, the *mind set* in which the dialogue between Islam and Christianity, and especially between Muslims and Franciscans should be conducted;[65] rather the exodus motif is also the *stuff*, the matter, this very dialogue is made of. As matter it constitutes a possible common ground between Islam and particularly Franciscanism, a *common ground* which is not primarily due to some occasional events, like St. Francis' visit to the sultan or other historical circumstances, but to the fact that the exodus gesture is part of the Islamo-Christian *faith structure itself.*[66]

Finally, a dialogue conducted in the name of the exodus motif inevitably leads to the following question: are *we* today still capable or willing to launch a new exodus, a new form of the "I do no longer adore what you adore!" as an answer to the burning problems of our time and as an attempt to keep both, Islam and Franciscanism, relevant also for

---

[62]Rule of 1221, chapter 9, *Omnibus*, 39.

[63]Mirror of Perfection, Chapter 18, *Omnibus*, 1143).

[64]Rule of 1221, chapter 23, *Omnibus*, 51.

[65]See my remarks in section one of this article.

[66]Again, this statement with regard to the structural level does not exclude differences on the level of content, i.e., with regard to the dogma.

the future? What is it that we have to leave behind, or have to break away from, if we embark on the road traced by our fathers in faith whose struggles and thoughts the present paper tried to bring closer to our heart and mind?

Bibliography

Feng, G.-F. and English, J. *Lao Tsu, Tao Te King*. Trans., New York, 1972.

Fontaine, I. C. *Futurité de l'Islam*. Tunis, 1972.

Francis of Assisi. *Writings and Early Biographies. English Omnibus of the Sources for the Life of St. Francis*, Ed. M.A. Habig. Quincy, IL: Franciscan University Press, 1991.

Hayek, M. *Les arabes et le baptême des larmes*. Paris, 1972.

—. *Le Mystère d'Ismaël*. Paris, 1959.

Lüling, G. *Die Wiederentdeckung des Propheten* Muḥammad. *Eine Kritik am "christlichen" Abendland*. Erlangen, 1981.

Mooren, T. *Es gibt keinen Gott — außer Gott. Der Islam in der Welt der Religionen*. Würzburg, Altenberge, 1996.

—. *Macht und Einsamkeit Gottes. Dialog mit dem islamischen Radikal-Monotheismus*. Würzburg, Altenberge, 1991.

— "Monotéisme coranique et anthopologie," *Anthropos*: St. Augustin 76 (1981): 529-561.

—. *On the Border — The Otherness of God and the Multiplicity of the Religions*. Frankfurt/M, 1994.

—. *Pengantar Agama Islam I. Islam. Pencaharian Identitas Orang Arab* (Introduction into Islam, in Indonesian language). Pematang Siantar, 1981.

Moubarac, Y. *Abraham dans le Coran. L'histoire d'Abraham dans le Coran et la naissance de l'Islam*, Paris, 1958.

Owomoyela, O. *Visions and Revisions. Essays on African Literatures and Criticism*. New York, 1991.

The Qur`ān. Trans. M.H. Shakir, M. H., New York, 1990 (Tahrike Tarsile Qur`ān).

Rodinson, M. *Mahomet*. Paris, 1961.

Talbi, M. *Islam et Dialogue. Réflexions sur un thème d'actualité*. Tunis, 1972.

Taubes, J. *Die politische Theologie des Paulus.* München, 1963.

Warren, H. C. *Buddhism in Translations.* Delhi, 1978. (reprint).

Wehr, H. *A Dictionary of Modern Written Arabic.* Ed. J. M. Cowan. Beirut/London, 1974. (reprint).

THE ARROGANCE OF OWNERSHIP

Environment and Economy
in Religious Focus

Anselm Moons, O.F.M., DD.

Introduction

Corrosive Self-interest

The extreme disregard for the environment, displayed by economists on the eve of the 21st century, justifies the fear that the Third Millennium will witness an armageddon with an uncertain outcome for both humanity and the entire universe. In a recent article[1] Lukas Vischer[2], addressing these issues of environment and economy, takes his starting point from the climatic change caused by human activities. Global mean surface temperature has increased by between about 0.3° and 0.6° C in the last hundred years. During the same period the global sea level rose between 10 and 25 cm. Climatic changes have highlighted concomitant dangers such as unnecessary oil consumption, deforestation, clean water shortages, floods, health hazards, damage to the earth's surface, air pollution.

Touching, amongst other issues, on the two sections of our article, economy and environment, the Swiss theologian asks whether humans in dealing with these two factors have a duty to recognize the rights of creation, i.e. animals, flowers, the elements

---

[1] L.Vischer, "Climate Change, Sustainability and Christian Witness," *The Ecumenical Review* 49 (1997):142-161.
[2] Emeritus professor of Ecumenism at the University of Bern, Switserland.

of nature? What are the limits of human responsibility? Vischer quotes H.E. Daly and J.B. Cobb who have spoken of "the corrosive effect of the individualistic self-interest."[3] They warn against the priority of the physical capital over the moral capital, because, in that situation the humans will fall victim to an unbridled and destructive self-interest[4].

Light from religion

A brief overview on how human owners have treated, in past and present, their fellow humans and the environment, the elements of creation, water — earth — air, will, hopefully, motivate Christian and Muslim alike to study and look closer at the disastrous consequences of this despicable and fatal behavior and compare it with words and deeds recorded in the two religions, viz. the Christian vision of Bible and Church tradition, and the Islamic teaching in Qur`ān and Hadith. The dissenting voice of Francis of Assisi in matters of property and ownership opens up the way to a Franciscan Ecology, the cornerstone of which will be Francis' conviction that humans are not the real owners of creation; they should pride themselves and shine in a conscientious stewardship, of that which really belongs to God alone.

I.

PROPERTY: THE ROOT OF ALL EVIL

1. Magnitude of the issue

Humans have been notorious for their desire to own both people and things. They wanted in their company a partner in life, children, relatives, and friends. But company alone proved

---

[3]H.E. Daly and J. Cobb, *For the Common Good: Redirecting the Economy towards the Community, the Environment and a Sustainable Future* (Boston,1989) 50f.

[4]Ruby Wax expressed the same tendency in this way: "*The selfish luxury of pursing moral principles!*"

insufficient. Humans, mostly men, wanted also to own them. In certain cultures, at certain times and places, men bought their wife and wives, bought women as concubines, bought slaves and catamites, sold them again at will and disposed of them in whatever way they liked. Humans often became spoils of war and property of the conqueror. Killing dependents was not unusual because, after all, they were only valued as property and not more than that!

Inhuman methods

Methods used to spend the minimum on and get the maximum out of their property led to very cruel and inhumane situations, neglect of property rented by third parties, forced labor for many hours a day[5], beating, torture, starvation and, on occasions, even killing. Slavery became common and wide-spread for many centuries. Age requirements were, for the sake of quick profit, mostly ignored. Child labor is practiced up to the present day in many countries throughout the world. The exploitation of children in the sex industry has taken on a global dimension and, even in the present time, keeps growing rapidly[6].

Besides fellow humans, men and women attach their sense of ownership also to things. Landowners are an early phenomenon of human history, although many primitive tribes detest the very thought[7]. Reverence and love of their native soil — as if it were

---

[5]Not only in many Third World countries are women's salaries a pittance, but even in rich European countries their salaries are 30 or 40% below those paid to men.

[6]Children are perhaps the easiest and greatest victims of human greed: too weak to defend themselves, too young to have voting power and their own income; children are underpaid, underfed (200 million go hungry all the time), under-educated (education often remains below 5% of the annual budget), easy targets for illegal business, handy soldiers in undercover activities, and daring streetfighters when law and order have broken down. The organs of babies — even unborn ones, and often along with poor mothers — are up for sale to serve the cosmetic and medical industry. India holds a world record of child labor with more than 80,000,000 boys and girls below the age of 14!

[7]Ownership of land led to ownership of both the produce and the work-force. The ownership of laborers led to enslavement. History reports that acquisition through ownership led to the craving for more without limits, including violence, force, conquest, war, robbery; if needed even with the help of superstition, religion, and self-made laws.

their own mother — make selling such land a genocidal crime to them. Land is acquired not only by individuals from relatives, friends, enemies, and whatever third parties, but also by corporate bodies, countries, multinationals, and other collective bodies.

Many-headed hydra

The colonial powers of the North brought bad times to their economically weaker brothers of the South. Using better weapons, more advanced techniques and scientific research, as well as faster means of transport, millions of Europeans indulged in genocidal practices for greater profit, dragged millions of blacks from their African homes for their new masters' economic manipulations: carting off raw materials and new sources of energy[8]. Frequently ignoring the rights and well-being of local people, vast differences have grown between <mostly white> colonizing and <mostly colored> colonized nations: 71.8% of the world population, residing in developing countries, enjoy only 18.6% of the GNP while the rich countries, with 28.2% of the peoples, claim 81.4% of the GNP! In the U.S., according to the IRS, the wealthiest 1% hold more than the bottom 90% combined[9].

Next, even in the recent past, big powers often drew artificial national boundaries for smaller nations, controlled their markets, at times prescribed one-sided crops, drafted arbitrary import and export regulations, collected unfair taxes, and imposed travel restrictions from the South to the North; in short, all evil signs and practices of unjust appropriation.

Misuse of natural resources is another consequence of the same claim to property. Exaggerated demands of greedy conquerors and desperate attempts of the defenders to halt them, have led to hundreds of wars and the killing of millions. Expert estimations suspect that up to 90% of the Aztecs, Mayas, and Quechua, or 20,000,000, lost their lives because of colonial pursuits. The craving for wealth and power of conquerors and warriors are even today

---

[8]Prof. F.C.Gerretson of the University of Utrecht wrote in the thirties that without the huge colonial windfall from Indonesia, the Netherlands would not have been more than a large ranch at the shores of the North Sea!

[9]Reported in *Sharings* XXVII, 4 (1997): 14.

causing exorbitant expenditures on all sorts of weaponry — conventional and nuclear.[10]

Finally, one more evidence of the many-headed hydra is the creation of the debt crisis of the Third World[11]. The Southern countries owe presently more than $2,000 billion to the rich countries in the North, which is $432, per person, or more than the average annual income of an African worker. It also means that the people today pay back about three times the amount their ancestors received in aid decades ago. In other words: today's poor have to pay a debt made by the previous generation. Still the rich countries remain reluctant to work out a solution of the same debt crisis for these poor countries in the Third World[12].

---

[10]Chernobyl has become a household word in nuclear discussions in Europe. This catastrophe is far bigger than either Ukraine or Russia can, of their own, afford to spend on repairing or rebuilding. A consortium of 15 countries, convened on November 20, 1997, by the UNO, offered to contribute $37 million to construct a new sacrophagus for reactor nr.4 which exploded in 1986. Earlier the G7 promised to contribute $300 million. The Ukraine government itself will pay $50 million. The total bill is estimated at $760 million.

[11]Most christian creditors, reciting the Lord's Prayer, *"Forgive our debtors,"* prefer a spiritual meaning of debt ignoring the Matthean material context which suggests that unmet taxes and unpaid loans must be let go. See M.W.D. Shomanah, "Praying the Lord's Prayer in a Global Economic Era." *The Ecumenical Review* IL (1997): 447.

[12] Not only poor countries are affected by unpayable debts. The latest cases concern two of the tiger countries of the Far East, until very recently much envied economic miracles: South Korea, the 11th economic power in the world, called on the I.M.F. for a loan of $60–70 billion, the biggest request since the application from Mexico three years ago. The first $20 billion have been promised but South Korea had applied for an extra $50 billion. Expert opinions about Korea's recovery vary from within a year or two to never ever...To help Indonesia paying its debt of more than $130 billion, the IMF promised a loan of $43 billion under the usual conditions. But when Indonesia threatened to delay the agreed upon reforms and, instead, opt for the system of *"currency board"*, thus stabilizing the rupiah by linking it to the US dollar, the I.M.F. withheld its first installment. Thereupon Indonesia stalled. After the fall of Soeharto, new negotiations with the I.M.F. have started. Japan's biggest stock-exchange, Yamaichi, declared bankruptcy. Soon after Japan landed in a financial crisis which led to a financial intervention by the U.S.A. to reinforce and stabilize the yen. These financial mishaps are partly due to unhealthy financial deals and manipulations of corrupt officials inspired by greed for quick and huge profit.The World Bank disagreed with the I.M.F.'s strategy. (J. Stiglitz in the *Wall Street Journal*, 1 August 1998.

The "Jubilee-2000" campaign[13] to forgive the debt of the poor countries, and the HIPC (Highly Indebted Poor Country) initiative have so far received a hesitant and lukewarm response from the creditors. Even the parallel or analogy between personal debtors and nations in debt has proved unconvincing: personal debtors, when bankrupt, can count on a release within a short time along with a new chance to fare better. Why not open up the same possibility for countries in debt[14]?

---

[13]Jubilee 2000 campaign has been launched by 2 lay christians, Martin Dent and Bill Peters. It is supported by Pope John Paul II in his letter, *Tertio Millennio Adveniente*, the CAFOD, and other aid agencies, including all Christian Churches in Britain. See R. Harris, "Forgive them their debts." *The Tablet* (20 September 1997): 1180. In 1998 500.000 signatures supporting the Jubilee 2000 campaign were presented to the G8-Heads of State in Birmingham, England. Germany will follow suit in 1999. Italy lends support to the Papal Campaign. The Secular Franciscans in Italy have started a similar campaign for signatures and call on the commissions for Peace and Justice in the whole Franciscan Order to do likewise. Campaigners compare their cause with the abolition of slavery in the 19th century. The Jubilee Campaign owes its name to the Biblical notion of Jubilee Year which itself has its roots in the legislation on the Sabbath in Exodus 23. This law prescribes that in the seventh year the land must lie fallow and its spontaneous produce is for the poor and the wild beasts. The seventh day, the sabbath, was taboo: according to Exodus all work had to be dropped. In Deuteronomy 'dropping' came to mean 'cancelling debts'. The order to desist from work was understood to come from the real owner of the land, God himself. Besides, the social concern for the poor plays a role. Disregard of the command and its double purpose led to the punishment of the exile. Deuteronomy will insist on the same two purposes of the sabbath: no work and no poor. "*There shall be no poor among you*" (Deut. 15:4). Whether the cancellation of debts replaced the 'impractical' fallow year or existed side by side, is debated. Lev. 25:14-17 insists upon honesty in buying and selling, care of the poor, and leaving the land uncultivated. Whether the laws of the Jubilee Year were properly observed is uncertain. Land cannot be sold in perpetuity and must remain available for redemption. Gradually the emphasis fell on the freeing of slaves, if they were fellow Israelites. To others, the law of the Jubilee Year was not applicable. The Jubilee Year reflects the belief in God as the owner of his land and his people. When Jesus refers to the Jubilee Year, he does not quote Leviticus, possibly because Jesus has a one time universal amnesty in mind. The liberation of which Jesus speaks is a "*total and a universal forgiveness of sins for all humankind.*" No one is excluded because all humans are brothers and sisters (Menezes, 668). See also F. Fox, "Rich man, poor man." *The Tablet* (4 October 1997): 1253.

[14]Africa is perhaps, of all continents, the worst victim of human greed. Millions of Africans were sold into slavery over many centuries by its near and distant neighbors, rulers, conquerors, masters, plunderers. Their territory is today threatened by a progressive desertification. Its land has often been the battleground of ideologies, competing political and economic powers.Between 1990 and 1995, Africa's share in the world trade dropped from 3.1% to 2.2%, although 730

Wide range of victims of greed

Objects of the greedy competitors are plentiful: oil in earth and water, fish in rivers, lakes and oceans, cattle in the fields, birds in the skies, trees in the rainforests[15]. In short, no place or creature escapes the greedy passion of the human owner[16]. The latest proof of this craving is the competitive exploration of outer space. The damage and harm of this uncontrolled hunt of energy and riches are high indeed:

- waste dumping causing severe air, soil and water pollution;
- uncontrolled desertification and deforestation leading to the expropriation of the first owners and, ultimately, the expulsion of local populations[17], land erosion, frequent shortages of firewood for the poor — or only at very long distances —, and flooding of rivers;
- unresolved threats from nuclear waste;
- the high risk of using plutonium in space industry;
- excessive wealth of a few versus dire poverty for the great majority.

---

million Africans represent 12% of the world population. Mozambique today is a poignant example of an economically bottomless pit in Africa. The average annual income of a Mozambican is US $90. It took the Club of Paris months to arrive at a debt relief of 80%. The Worldbank and the I.M.F. had in vain asked for a relief of 90%. Japan and Germany refused. Mozambique's good behavior must first entitle her to more aid. The country has just come out of a long and disastrous civil war; allotments for health is 6.2% and education is only 4.4%. In 1994 the Asian-Africa Forum was far more optimistic about Africa's share in the economic growth than present conditions justify.

[15]US national forests, once a limitless resource, are dwindling due to wrong political decisions. Examples: the great Tongass National Forest in SE Alaska; three forests in N. California; road-building programs in forests. See editorial of *The Washington Post* in *Herald Tribune* 28 October 1997.

[16]For thoughtless people the earth is not more than both a store-house and a dump. Feminists see parallels between these attitudes the way in which women and the earth are treated. See A. Grond, *Moeder Natuur en haar recalcitrante dochters. Een feministische stem in het milieudebat* (J.v.Arkel, Utrecht, 1998), 20.

[17]In 1996, 140,827 cases of violent action against Indians in Brasil, esp. the *Yanomani*, the *Guarani*, the *Tapeba* and the *Nambikwara*, have been recorded (an increase of 92% compared to 1995). Bodily injuries increased by 62%. Suicides augmented with 34%. See *Missionsdienst*, Missionszentrale der Franziskaner, Bonn, Germany, February 1998.

- disproportion of resources and opportunities for the rich and the poor[18].

Gains and losses?

The enormity of these abuses evokes the question whether the states or the national governments have taken steps to prevent or stop these exploitations? Hardly; Sweden would have liked to. Against those countries — like Argentina — who tried, financial manipulations against their currency and national budget deficits were applied to break their resistance. Other countries, especially the strongly industrial ones, have initiated economic pressures favoring the capitalist markets, and stalling political, social and ecological progress. From then on the global economy[19] was led by Transnational Corporations (TNC) which - with the help of free banking zones — could freely manipulate interest rates, speculation, and tax flight. They received further support from the Structural Adjustment Programs (SAP) which favored capital owners over the working and socially dependent majorities. The worldwide debt crisis, mainly caused by capitalists, individuals and collective bodies, eager to escape high taxes, started from the South and affected all but the host countries of the capital flight. Naturally, debts have to be paid; with the awful consequence of further impoverishment due to austerity drives, but thereby disguising the real and obvious aim

---

[18]Government policies, with market economics, give all priority to profit making and stimuli for more production. Such policy very frequently hurts recipients of benefits like senior citizens, unskilled and low pay job holders. In the Netherlands, in the eighties, the distance between the rich and the poor increased by 22.5%: the 20% poorest of the Dutch could spend 10% less while the richest 20% of the population enjoyed an increase of wealth of 12.5%. In 1994, Duchrow reports, the German owners of capital enjoyed an increase of 9.1%. But net wages and salaries went up by 0.2%, available jobs went down by 1.2% and unemployment payments were lowered by 4.4%. Conclusion: *"within the structures of globalized capital markets, growth is killing jobs."* Duchrow, "God or Mammon: economics in conflict." *Mission Studies* XIII (1996): 34-35.

[19]The global economic order was launched at the Bretton Woods Conference in 1944, at a time when the USA was the only economic superpower. See also PP. John XXIII, *Peace on Earth* (1963)130; *Economic Justice for All,* (1986) nos.10-13;113-116;231;251-292;322-325. The First All-American Bishops' 1997 Synod in Rome made the global economy one of its major themes.

of "privatizing gains and socializing losses".[20] The helping hand of political bodies was further strengthened by dictatorial powers suppressing social counter-movements, at times even by direct military interventions, strategies of Low Intensity Conflicts, disinformation campaigns, and control of transnational communication channels feeding and misinforming popular views and dreams.

A voice from the Third World

In a recent interview Tissa Balasuriya summarized this historic development as follows: "For five hundred years nothing but myths! At least, that is what I have learned from history. The European white population started growing after they had discovered new land, let's say from 1492 (Christopher Columbus) and 1498 (Vasco da Gama). Hardly any country in the world was spared this European dominance. Traces of white invasion are found everywhere. In cases a country was not occupied, its market was put firmly under control. Raw materials were hauled off, cultures were subdued, peoples massacred. Australia and Canada are cases in point. Such behavior results in debts? Not really! The white man has arranged matters in such a way that, after his colonial looting, he then manages to become the creditor of these same colonized countries. This manipulation forces the colonized people to go along with the free market strategy, selling off its raw materials, tolerating environmental pollution. 'The earth stinks, the sea is dying, the air is filthy, the sun obscured by smoke'. Yet, the white man still goes wherever he wants, makes children whenever he desires. Meanwhile the Chinese is chained and fettered within his own borders and must be satisfied with one child only. The African is not allowed to leave his country, Europe closes its borders. Meanwhile the goods traffic must be free and made available for shipping the world over, a freedom supervised and guaranteed by the U.N.O. In this manner the world passes its death sentence over Africa which, over and above, is threatened by a fatal desertification. Earlier in history Africans were worth their weight in gold! As slaves they were economic merchandise. This historic imbalance must be rectified,

---

[20]Duchrow, 37-38.

and today, five hundred years after Vasco da Gama, the rich world of the North must settle its debts to the countries of the South."[21]

2. Theological Identification

Interpretations vary depending on the angle from where the issue is approached.

First of all, Buddha approached the issue from the natural point of view and thought that the human desire constituted the principal threat to all life on earth.

Secondly, Rudolf Bahro[22], an author of our own times, looks toward the religious dimension and suspects that the world religions are the cause of the ecological crisis, the christian tradition in particular. Michel Camdessus, general director of the I.M.F., on the other hand, advances again another religious world view: he sees in the global economy the favorite way to the Kingdom of God. It will create enough wealth to effectively help the poor[23]. It almost sounds like the language of liberation theology. Religious groups reject the opinion of Camdessus, even though as a christian, his attention is turned to God and not to the idol of the Mammon.

Christians and Muslims alike reject any worship of idols. They simply consider idolatry the greatest offense humans can commit. Besides, next to the first sinful deed, Christians read in Holy Scripture indications of an "original sinfulness" which is considered inherent and innate. This sinful condition is by birth common to all of Adam and Eve's children. St. Paul's words *"sin came into the world through one human"*(Romans 5,12), together with the human and theological experience of St. Augustine, have given a definitive direction to the acceptance of this biblical and theological tradition.

---

[21]T. Balasuriya, "For sanity." in *Jeevadhara* XXV, No. 147 (1995), 38.

[22]See R. Bahro, *Die Logik der Rettung*, s.d.

[23]In a special issue of *The Times Literary Supplement*, entitled *Social Studies*, Zygment Bauman analyses the social usefulness of the poor in rich countries. In times past the rich used the poor as receivers of alms given to please God. Nor can today's poor serve any more as wood-cutters and water-carriers; or be available as a standby-labor force. They surely cannot stimulate our modern economy as consumers. In a word, the poor are useless, superfluous; rather unwanted guests in a flourishing economy.

Adam's fall

The historical existence of Adam as well as his sinful behavior in paradise have been the subject of frequent and profound theological reflections throughout the history of christian theology. The tale of the apple between Eve and Adam — which has given occasion to much injustice and harm to women — is now widely recognized as being just that, a tale. Evolution theories also call for a very cautious approach to the historical character of the events in the first paradise. On the other hand, there is amongst humans a widespread conviction that things are not right and have, throughout human history, never been right. In various stories of different cultures we read of humans in search of something which seems lost. From all sides people are thought to be en route to return to the original place where things once were right for everyone; the ineradicable dream of utopia. However, the answers as to why things today are not right differ greatly.

Theologians have often tried to qualify the nature of this turning away from God, on the base of the paradise story itself. Was it the desire to be equal to God? Was it the thirst for <unbecoming> knowledge? Or was it the first experience of an uncontrolled sexual desire? Many theologians opt for a safer and more sober answer. Adam disobeyed God and dragged his posterity with him into a condition of enmity with God.

Such an answer may not satisfy everyone. In any case, it did not satisfy Francis of Assisi either, to whom Adam's "disobedience" did not seem the full story. Francis looked for a more concrete form which this disobedience took. Where do we see this fundamental sinfulness at work? In what behavior does this 'natural' inclination to sin become visible most clearly?

For our article the answer of Francis is, of course, of special interest. However, before we look closer into Francis' texts, we focus on what are considered usual viewpoints in matters of property, both inside and outside of the Catholic tradition.

II.

RANDOM REMARKS ON OWNERSHIP

1. Secular Views

For many humans who, in most of their desires and activities, are craving to "have and have ever more", it is obvious that they have a right to own and to govern what they consider their property. Besides protecting one's personal freedom, property, it is maintained, strengthens one's self-worth, guarantees one's safety and provides the necessary tools to work and to earn. Property also enables persons to further enlarge their property. To safeguard this personal property, an extensive system of legislation has been worked out in the course of centuries. It is significant to remark that this legislation, guaranteeing one's possessions, have not been made by have-nots but, of course (!), by those who already have and feel the need to protect their possessions with effective laws. At best, the have-nots are offered a minimum salary and/or given the promise that they may count on the kindhearted generosity of individuals and charitable organizations. In fact, many of these take pride in their charitable contributions and from time to time donate large sums of money to different causes.

Stocks and heritage

Then, the more one has, the more one can acquire. One way is through financial dealings such as investments[24], buying and selling stocks and bonds, etc. The laws of succession are another case in point. They firmly protect the family–property, and, even though modern states do often attempt to limit these rights, most of this wealth goes directly from parents to children and relatives, even before these children reach the age to handle and use it themselves. The disadvantage of poor people's progeny is obvious: children of

---

[24]'Ethical Investments' are a recent development: a list of companies is available and kept up-to-date by experts which promote the environment, a respect for the social climate, and the care of animals. Those which invest in oil, weapons, nuclear energy are excluded from this list. The attitude of both, investors and companies, towards human rights, is as yet in discussion.

the poor remain as poor when their relatives die. This inequality between children constitutes an injustice with big consequences for their future. Again, the question of who made these laws of succession need not be asked: the testator wants his inheritance to be transferred integrally to his children and relatives.

Without limits

While feeble attempts have been made to secure a minimum existence for all, most of them have proved ineffective. On the other hand, no limits have ever been put by any authority to the maximum that individuals or corporate bodies may own. The number of millionaires[25] in the USA is no longer recorded or published while the number of billionaires is growing rapidly. Last year alone there was a 25% increase in their number. In 1998 it was estimated that Bill Gates himself had more than 36 billion dollars[26]. He recently declared to see himself as steward rather than as owner and might follow the example of tycoon Ted Turner whose fresh donation of 1 billion dollars to the United Nations [27] is unusual. Most donations are meant to be paid out only after death. Meanwhile, thirty five million Americans are financially unable to insure themselves or their family. People who cannot pay their rent are put out on the street. Many of them have nowhere to live but in their car. This immense gap is rationally and socially explained as a regrettable but unavoidable side effect of market economy and

---

[25]In the presence of billionaires, millionaires like to refer to themselves as *"simple millionaires"!*

[26]His many adversaries refer to Microsoft as the 'Evil Empire' which gobbles up all budding competitors. On January 13, 2000, the day Bill Gates at age 44, the wealthiest man in the world, announced his resignation as the president of Microsoft. At that time his personal wealth was estimated to be between 80 and 100 billion dollars.

[27]Earlier gifts of Turner, sometimes called *Mouth of the South*, were meant to support environmental projects and birth control programs. Urged on by his conviction that *"we live together on this planet"*, this new gift is to be directed towards the elimination of landmines, eradication of diseases, and the welfare of children and refugees. He reported that he had earned this one billion dollars in a period of nine months. He encouraged other "super-rich" to do the same. No wonder, the CNN impact on news is *not only reporting news but making news and policies too!*

liberalization of the world market.[28] The cry that the rich get richer and the poor get poorer[29] is for them no cause for alarm but listened to with resignation and mostly ignored[30]. A similar gap exists between the rich nations in the First World and the poorer ones in the Third World[31]. For the latter a globalized economy has not yet

---

[28]The gap between rich and poor happens because "...Capital markets have been globalized while the countervailing power of organized labor has been kept fragmented." Duchrow, 36. "Globalization brings as many serious disadvantages for the poor as did the Victorians' pioneering colonial mission..Globalization represents the acceleration of the destructive features of advanced capitalism." P. Vallely and I. Linden, "The Tide can be tamed. Doing battle with globalization." *The Tablet* (16 August 1997) 1034.

[29]The crucial question, whether enriching **causes** impoverishment, is rarely taken up and never answered. At best, partial answers are volunteered such as: tax dodging shifts the burden to the weaker members of society. Large scale speculations on the money market lead to heavier burdens for the average citizen: less capital, higher interests, higher rents.

[30]In recent years, however, fresh efforts to turn around the scourge of unemployment are noticeable.Within the last five years, the USA has brought down their percentage from 7% to 5%. Europe is still hesitant to agree to a joint approach, with the excuse that national causes and treatments are considered too different. Until now, they are planning to formulate common targets and annual reporting on their efforts and results to reduce the number of 18 million unemployed by 12 million, i.e., from 11% to 7% of the whole workforce, whereas at present the annual increase of unemployed is about 2 million workers. In Spain the unemployment is 20%, the highest in the whole of the European Union. Of the 18 million unemployed, 5 million are below the age of 25. Among the proposed measures to reduce the number of unemployed are: to teach laborers new skills, and to restructure certain regulations, e.g., for hiring and firing workers. Social guarantees for workers have been suggested by the new social government of Tony Blair in Britain — in contrast with their conservative predecessor — at the November 1997 meeting of European governments in Luxembourg.

[31]The International Monetary Fund (I.M.F.) — which presently operates with a capital of 285 million dollars — welcomed its new mandate spelled out in the *"Declaration of Hong Kong"* of September 1997. In spite of the hesitations of the developing countries, this declaration authorizes the I.M.F. to *"orderly"* liberalize the movement of capital. This new mandate inaugurates the I.M.F. as the *police force* of the world economy! In the future, countries will need permission from the I.M.F. to impose restrictions on this movement of capital. The aim is complete liberalization of any capital flow between all countries. Restrictions still regulate quantities of capital flow, taxes, and subsidies on this flow, and the national exchange rates. Experts fear that with the new role of the I.M.F. the distinction between supporting local governments and interference in their internal affairs has become a very *"thin line."* The *Wall Street Journal* recently published a very different view on the I.M.F. in an article signed by prominent personalities: former ministers George Schultz, William Wriston and the top banker William Simon, who

proved to be a blessing. The "trickling effect" of the market economy is still an empty promise or tempting mirage[32].

2. Catholic Position

To a large extent the Catholic Church is in agreement with the secular views on property. However, there are important nuances. The existence of God is a basic element of the Christian teaching on property: all things are created by God. This makes God the owner of all things[33] who has given stewardship of his creation to

---

are of the opinion that the I.M.F. is ineffective, superfluous, and outdated! According to them, the saving efforts of the I.M.F. obstruct the free flow of supply and demand in the global market, unduly protect Asian investments by banks with tax-payers' money, shield corrupt dictators against their enemies, and is itself not open to criticism. In response, the I.M.F. president M.Camdessus proposes the following reforms: (1) more supervision and information about economic policies of countries; (2) sharper regional control and cooperation; (3) better ways of involving the private sector in crisis control; (4) better prevention of easy loans by the banks; (5) controlled liberalization of the international flow of capital; (6) reinforcing of international institutions by reinforcing their capital; (7) combatting all corruption. The American Congress and Alan Greenspan have their own reasons to foster reservations towards the I.M.F.

[32]Many experts fear that global integration will result in local disintegration. In 1990 Africa received only 5% of the *Foreign Direct Investment* worldwide; most of the 5% went to South Africa alone. Of the 53 African countries, 48 saw scarcely any cash. The conclusion has been drawn that *"perhaps half of the world's population is now virtually written off as far as foreign investors are concerned."* George Soros put it recently this way: *"Untrammeled intensification of laissez-faire capitalism and the spread of market values into all areas of life is undermining social values of morality."*

[33]This view is common in the patristic times (AD 150-650). A few relevant quotations, some of them taken from Th. Cullinan:

St. Clement of Alexandria (AD 150-215): *"have what you need; all other goods are meant for sharing. You don't need your silver urinals and chamber pots of transparent alabaster."*

St. Ambrose of Milan (AD 333-397): *"Not from your own do you bestow upon the poor man, you return what is his. For what has been given as common for the use of all, you appropriate to yourself alone. The earth belongs to all, not to the rich...You are therefore paying a debt, not bestowing a bounty."* An absolute right to own, Ambrose says, is idolatry. To measure what you own, look at your need and the purpose for what you need it. One of his favorite images in matters of ownership is one's nakedness in womb and tomb: in neither place there is room for more than yourself. Also: *"precious ornaments delight you, although others do not even have grain...The jewel in your ring could save the lives of a whole people."*

St. Basil the Great of Cappadocia (AD 330-379), one of the Cappadocean Fathers, also called Basil of Caesarea: *" 'Whom do I injure' (says the rich person),*

the humans. Yet, simultaneous, it is explicitly and officially stated that private property is a divinely ordained right of the individual[34]. This right of the individual must at all times be reconciled, on the one hand, with the demands of the Common Good of society, and, on the other hand, with the care of the needy and the oppressed for the simple reason that God, being just, sides with the poor and weak in society. We hear this out of the mouths of the prophets and of Jesus himself. Besides, God liberates his oppressed people out of Egypt, freeing them from debt and slavery. Christians read these divine interventions as authentic signs of God's love for the humans. Recent popes and bishops, amongst them the US hierarchy, echo this biblical teaching stating that the right to private property does not include the superfluous when others still lack necessities. However, the superficial examples given and the failure to repeatedly insist on implementation, suggest a rather lukewarm commitment.

---

when I retain and conserve my own? Which things, tell me, are 'yours'? When have you brought them into being?...Because the rich were first to occupy common goods, they take these goods as their own. If each would take what is sufficient for one's needs, leaving what is in excess to those in distress, no one would be rich, no one poor." Basil compares having a surplus to occupying a seat in a theater and preventing someone else from coming in. Also: the right to land equals the right to the air one breathes.

St. Augustine of Hippo (AD 354-430): *"We possess many superfluous things, unless we keep only what we need. And once we seek what we don't need, nothing ever suffices...so consider: not only do you need few things, but God himself does not require you to answer for many things. Therefore look at what he has given you and take from that what you need; other things, superfluous things, are the basic necessities of others. The superfluities of the wealthy are the necessities of the poor; so their possession is that of other people's property."*

[34]It should be reported that discussions to improve the position of the poor have begun challenging the — until now — unassailable position of the rich. There is a renewed desire to look into the *"problem of the rich."* The rights of the poor must affect the position of the rich. Religions should offer materials on profit making, financial speculations, and the like for discussion. Some suggest that those who refuse to review the dividing lines between rich and poor, lose their rights to make further use of public services and ought to restrict themselves to private services. Others offer a new criterium: The net biggest income should not exceed five times the net lowest income. This criterium should, according to this opinion, be made the guiding principle both in business and in one's private life.

Currents and influences

Meanwhile, an increasing number of Christian authors and leaders promote the market economy, the idol of our times, and do little or nothing to fight or abolish the growing world poverty. Self-interest remains for most economists an accepted powerful motor of the economy. Occasionally, critics ask whether increasing one's wealth must be measured by the amount of labor put in by the new owner him/herself. For many even raising this moral question breathes the spirit of days gone by: receiving interest, buying and selling shares and stocks, involve little or no labor while the increase in personal wealth can be exorbitant: in 1996 for some it was between 26 and 52%! Or is this profit perhaps to be called usury, by virtue of the outdated (?) dictum that "money should not make money"...?

Catholic reflections in the course of this century have mostly been developed in the context of the industrial relationship between employer and employee. Issues such as just salary, family wages, and trade unions are therefore frequently discussed in the documents of that period. Also, whatever the importance of economic development, other values such as social progress and human freedom had to be integrated as well. In short, the Church tried to steer a course between the conflicting demands of liberalism and capitalism on the one hand, and the threat from systems of communism and fascism on the other.[35]

After World War II, and even more so after the Second Vatican Council (1962-1965), Catholic teaching on property started showing a greater affinity with an evolutionary understanding of the world. John XXIII noticed that "our times are marked by a pronounced

---

[35]M. Novak seeks reconciliation between the Catholic social doctrine and the free market economy. The historic capitalism is a typical product of the Jewish-Christian tradition. Novak is convinced that his liberal economic theology is in accordance with the teaching of John Paul's Encyclical, *Centesimus Annus*, which stresses the creative subjectivity of the free woman and man at work. Democratic capitalism is, according to Novak, an economic order of superior quality and a true revolution of the spirit. Modern enterprises are called by Novak an incarnation of God's presence and signs of Grace! Market economy is social because it brings people from all walks of life together who can then decide, in a joint approach, on the models of their strategy. The free market process produces prosperity and well-being, with the ultimate aim to abolish all poverty in the world.

dynamism."[36] Historical movements began to take priority over philosophical teaching. Also the global context starts replacing an exclusively western one. One of the new priorities in modern thinking will therefore be the global equality which as yet remains a far away dream. In more than one way the macro economy constitutes a rival and threat to the micro economy. Individual persons — especially the poor —, institutions, and local conditions risk being overlooked or underestimated. The environment is a prominent one amongst these particular interests. But in spite of the increasing frequency and importance of worldwide consultations on the environment, the global economy succeeds in taking first place.

Perspective of a Biblical Third Way

Meanwhile, the Common Good theory remains a major guideline in Catholic teaching on the future world order, including property and appropriation.[37] Duchrow[38] pleads, therefore, for a sociological analysis of Bible texts to detect their social context: socio-economic and political structures and actions are, from the biblical perspective, decisions for or against God. A theological vision on social issues is the only way to neutralize the secularization of God, says Duchrow.[39] The same vision also offers a basis for the growing interest in an alternative economy - a third way between capitalism and socialism -. The alternative economy is an *Economy of the Sufficient*, which slows down the consumer's cry for ever more

---

[36]The Lutheran Ulrich Duchrow, professor in Heidelberg, opposes neo-Lutherans' interpretation of Luther's *two kingdom theory*, according to which politics and economy are seen as autonomous and independent of faith. Luther, Duchrow maintains, keeps politics/economy and faith/church interrelated.

[37]Duchrow sees a link between a neo-liberal world capitalism and such phenomena such as poverty, environmental pollution and oppression, because this economic system aims primarily at financial profit instead of answering basic need. Money produces an accumulation of wealth rather than serving as a medium of exchange. See Noordergraaf, "Ulrich Duchrow: Een belijdende Kerk in verzet tegen het mondiale kapitalisme." *Riding the Juggernaut*, 33.

[38]Duchrow is program coordinator of **Kairos Europa** which promotes an intercontinental network of marginalized individuals and groups which cooperate with NGOs and Church organizations to fight for more economic, social, racial and gender justice.

[39]Noordergraaf, 33.

and creates space for the needs of the poor, better social care, improvement of labor conditions, care for the environment, and a more rationalized use of energy.

3. The Islamic Economic System[40]

In accordance with the purpose of this publication, next to the secular view and the Catholic position on property and appropriation, the Islamic views and practices are here briefly summarized and placed in perspective.

No Third Way

The late Mawlana Mawdudi[41], a leading politician and renowned Islamic scholar in Pakistan, opted for a theocratic political system because no human being can be expected to draft laws free from all selfishness. Mawdudi, therefore, could not support the optimistic view that an Islamic economic system could ever offer a valid and viable Third Way between capitalism and socialism. Islam does not present an alternative but has developed an independent system with its focus on the well-being and security of all members of the *Umma*, the ideal community for which the first *Umma* of Medina remains the inspiration. Guided by the recognition of Divine Sovereignty on the one hand, and a human stewardship of property on the other, wealth and riches of the individual are ethically acceptable, provided the wealthy fulfil their obligation to share their surplus with the near and weak ones in society: the marital

---

[40]P. Robert, *The issue of dehumanizing poverty in the Indian Subcontinent. An Islamic and Catholic Perspective*, 2 vols. (1997), 110-124; J. Waardenburg, *Islam. Norm en werkelijkheid*, (Antwerpen, 1984), 349-365; H. Driessen, a.o. *In het huis van de Islam.* (Nijmegen, 1997), 347-360.

[41]Sayyid Abu 'L-A'LA Mawdudi (1903-1979), religious leader and founder of the *Jamaat-i-Islami*, a political party in Pakistan which from 1941 onward fought for an independent Islamic State, built his movement on the Sacred Texts and, with that foundation, presented his Party of God as the best and only possible for all times and all places. The reform had to come from the top, the leadership first. It was to be the first step towards the Islamic State with the _Shariah_ as the deciding authority. The Prophet Moḥammad was simultaneously religious leader, head of the Islamic State, military commander, and chief judge. The first basic principles of the Islamic State are the Sovereignty of God and the Authority of the Prophet.

partner, parents, children, heirs, the poor, the old, women, slaves, refugees, pilgrims, soldiers, converts. Social and religious institutes too can count on special support from the rich. The following are examples of how the Islamic society cares for its members.

Rights of succession

Next to the criminal law, the laws and rights of succession are amongst the most extensive in Islam. The Qur`ān provides detailed specifics which are sacred and widely observed. Debts of the deceased are not included in the inheritance laws. Affinity and gender are primary criteria in the laws of succession. Usually women inherit only half of their male counterpart. In order to safeguard and keep the inheritance as a unit intact, not everyone is easily ready to pay out to women their rightful share of the succession.

Waqf

A frequent method to circumvent payment to women is to establish a fund for a religious foundation which is called *Waqf*. *Waqf* (or *habous*) protects the continuation of the family property against an unwanted division of the inheritance. Nor can the state confiscate the *Waqf*. The proceeds of *Waqf* go to religious or charitable purposes. Specifications of this purpose make allowance for gifts to relatives. Sometimes the proceeds remain with the founder and his own descendants. This financial clout gave the *Waqf* a considerable political independence from state authorities. They often exercised a very good influence on the larger society. However, with the passing of time and change of circumstances, *Awqaf* did lose most of their influence, often due to poor management by underpaid officials and occasional conservative elements in the administration. In 1924 secularized Turkey closed them all down, followed by Egypt in 1952, and Tunisia in 1956.

Mahr Sadâq

Moḥammad's efforts to improve the social position of women are well known and appreciated. One of his ways to do this was the introduction of the bridal gift, *Mahr/Sadâq*, by the future bridegroom. It must be noted that this gift was not a payment to

the bride's father but to the bride herself, often in two install-
ments. It gave women some social independence and status, as they
themselves could make certain expenses, and develop social contacts
through small gifts and purchases. Tradition fixed a minimum limit
but never laid down a maximum to the *Mahr*.

Zakât

Another very important measure to take care of the economically
weaker ones was the introduction of the *Zakât* (alms)[42]. *Zakât* is one
of the Five Pillars of Islam, and one of the most important ritual
obligations of a Muslim. It has also become an essential element of
the Islamic economy. *Zakât* is a form of compulsory tax by which
the Muslim, for the love of Allah, alleviates the burden of the poor,
orphans, and prisoners. It gives ritual purity to the donor who at the
same time gathers more merits for paradise. Mohammad himself
mentioned among the beneficiaries, beside those just referred to:
the *Zakât* officials, recent converts, slaves, debtors, travellers and
soldiers who fight for God's cause. Mohammad's successor, Abu
Bakr, determined the percentages: 10% for landed property (*'ushr*)
and 2% for all other property. In addition to this tax there is the
Zakât al-fitr which is paid during the month of *Ramadân*, a mostly
symbolic amount paid to the mosque for the poor and needy. The
Zakât strengthens the financial position of the *Umma* and
demonstrates a sense of social responsibility. Later forms of taxes
have weakened the commitment to the *Zakât*. Recently there is a
spiritual revival and return to the observance of this basic principle
of Islam, often in combination with the introduction of the *Shariah*,
both of which are also favored by fundamentalistic movements.

---

[42]*Zakât* legislation has been introduced in Saudi-Arabia (1951), Lybia (1971),
Pakistan (1980) and Sudan (1984). For certain Muslims the collecting of this
religious tax by the State makes the religious character of the obligation doubtful.
Migrants often transfer their payment to their country of origin.

Sadaqa

Next to the *Zakât*, the Muslim pays yet another tax, the *Sadaqa*.[43] This tax is a voluntary and meritorious (*baraka*) tax. Gifts in kind are particularly popular among the women, like providing meals for the poor, and sharing the meat of sacrificial animals, sweets and nuts. These are distributed at public places, such as mosques and cemeteries. This *Sadaqa* expresses and demonstrates the eagerness to share with one another, and can never be refused. Refusal destroys the relationship with the donor and the *Baraka*.

Riba

Riba (interest)[44] is another financial transaction which is typical for the Islam. A good Muslim should not make money from money. For a Muslim all 'money from money' is sinful usury and, therefore, to be ruled out in an Islamic economy. For non-Islamic economic systems a "reasonable" interest is practiced and considered legitimate. In a multi-cultural and multi-religious international society that constitutes a problem. For the Muslim businessman or woman the way out of this dilemma is sharing in the risk of a particular project through participation in its loss and profit. Islamic banking follows this model: one party invests the capital, the other provides for expertise and labor. In Islamic banking the former is a limited partner and not a creditor. Smart banking ought to avoid major fluctuations in dividend. To do so, the bank will draw the dividend from one project and spread the payment of dividend out over a number of years.[45] Experience has shown that with this procedure the two amounts of interest and of profit-sharing come about even.

---

[43] In Egypt, a growing number of business people invest voluntary donations to improve the position of the poor by providing them with housing, work, etc., to offer an alternative, a third way, in order to bring the stalemate between government and fundamentalists to a peaceful solution.

[44] The prohibition of the *Shariah* to take interest has become law in Lybia (1971), Sudan (1983), Iran (1983), Pakistan (1984). A ruling of the Pakistani Federal Shariah Court in 1991 has been suspended.

[45] The largest Islamic Bank is the *Daar al-Maal al-Islami* (D.M.I.) with most of the initial capital from Saudi Arabia. Its daughter bank, the *Islamic Takaful Company*, has expanded its operations to Europe.

The principal intentions of Islamic banking are twofold: firstly, not to use money without spending productive energy; secondly, to practice Islamic banking with due respect of the social responsibility of the state. The state must keep the market forces under control to secure the national resources or riches. Then also a fair share in decent living can be guaranteed for the poorest of the poor.[46]

Assessment

To bring this brief summary of Islamic teachings and practices on property and appropriation to a close, the following observations seem pertinent. Firstly, the Prophet Moḥammad was strongly motivated and took courageous and concrete steps to care for the weaker ones in the society of his days. His successor followed in his footsteps, as did so many of his followers.

Secondly, social concerns also became a hallmark of the Islamic movement based on definite instructions of the Holy Book of Qur`ān which for Muslims are binding to the hilt. The Christians take pride in their love of God and neighbor as their First Commandment, but are often poorly informed about this very sympathetic and human side of the Islamic faith. Efforts towards religious collaboration in this area of charity, if they exist, are not recorded.

Thirdly, Islamic banking presupposes well intentioned capitalists with a strong social sense of responsibility of the state which must protect the resources of the nation and not give in to the pressure of the world market. At the same time the state must guarantee a decent living for the weaker ones. The system is said to work best with an authoritative, paternalistic government which allows the economic and industrial forces lots of leeway. It seems significant that Pakistan introduced the Islamic banking system but did not apply the Islamic banking system to its own dealings with

---

[46]The 'oil-states' receive, of course, themselves big revenues from which they can support the new system but with the disadvantage that their income is very one-sided. Third World countries, on the other hand, have little income and will have to silence their social consciousness for a long time to come.

other countries, and, at home, continued to issue state loans carrying the usual practice of paying out interest.

Fourthly, in practice the state needed more revenues than the original arrangements had made allowance for which had counted on a regular income from spoils of war. In history, many tribes refused to pay, considering this income illegitimate. Tribal chiefs and large landowners felt strong enough not to comply with the obligation. It must therefore be admitted that lofty intentions towards the poor and needy in Islamic banking do not by themselves guarantee the success of this new banking system.

In conclusion, we think that the substructure in the days of the Prophet were really unprepared for the new experiment: the state was a weak entity overpowered by dominant family ties, rich landlords and influential tribal leaders. The royal court itself was a small unit supported by soldiers, ready to conquer whatever was assigned to them, and who lived off their spoils of war. Similar obstacles exist in our present times where power centers, such as multinationals, global economies, and international banking seem to outwit the best of human ideals.

People, Muslims and others, can be selfish and take advantage of their fellow human beings. The measures Moḥammad took to protect the women brides in Islamic families proved insufficient. The *waqf* too fell victim of its own good intentions to help the needy and were subsequently put out of business by modern states. Even one of the pillars of Islam, the *zakât*, experienced a steep decline over a long period of time. The multinationals are the power centers of today's economy and the market economy dictates economic and social decisions of the modern state. With the unfortunate consequence that Divine Instructions and lofty human ideals are kept at bay.

4. Environmental Rape

A. *The Fazendeiros and 'Os Sem Terra'*

The human thirst for property is unquenchable. The worst form is surely the audacity to rob fellow human beings of their fundamental right of freedom. Earlier in this article we have listed the various abuses that "owners" have allowed themselves towards other humans. For rural people land and environment are matters of life and death. Yet this lifeline is often very brittle and fragile. In Brasil '*Os Sem Terra*' (landless people) have begun to protest against landowners, *Fazendeiros*, who leave their land fallow rather than to make it available for peasants whom the government has promised land to live on. The first protest of about 8,000 'landless' resulted in 20 of them being killed. They were a gathering of riff-raff from the city, left-overs from the rural economy, day laborers without work, discharged factory and construction workers, farmers' sons, failed students, and phased-out civil servants. In all there are about one million of them, according to government sources. In 1996, the *Movimento Sem Terra* organized 176 land-occupations in which 45,218 families took part. '*Os Sem Terra*' face many hardships: too little to eat, their sick not welcome at hospitals, and constant harassment by local people. "We are waiting for God to free the hearts of the rich", says one of '*Os Sem Terra*'. Their leaders, supported by the recently created Cardinal Serafim Fernandes, wonder how the free market economy will obstruct their efforts to make '*Os Sem Terra*' landowners, if they are ever to see that dream come true. The *Movimento Sem Terra*, initiated by the Church twenty years ago, is a present-day echo of Emiliano Zapata, animator of the Mexican revolution, who in 1911 used to say: "*La tierra es de quien la trabaja.*"

B. The Environment

Another victim of the environmental rape is the environment itself and the suffering it received from the arrogance of its human "owner." The human owner, a 'Johnny-come-lately" who arrived only 300,000 years ago, feels and behaves like 'King of the Universe'; a view hardly supported by the much longer lifespan, greater endurance and overall superiority of the whole universe[47]. Today's specialization and fragmentation, however, have misled

---

[47]See S. J. Gould, *Full House*, 1997.

humans to consider themselves the principal part of the greater universe[48] which began its own course 15 billion years ago[49].

The mutual relationship between all-natural elements and animated inhabitants should make humans more respectful and humble towards all fellow elements and inhabitants. All share one common life, all contribute to the whole in their own inimitable way.

However, none of this worldview inspires the human behavior. On the contrary, convinced and proud of their own kingship, humans seek to take out from nature whatever they can[50]. The damage that humanity has done, and daily continues doing, defies any adequate description. A few facts will serve to illustrate this point.

Eco-fascism?

Natural disasters, especially in the Third World, are a case in point. The developing world cannot yet afford, on its own, to build adequate resistance against these calamities and bring under control severe cold, extreme heat, torrential rains, floods, tidal waves, earthquakes and serious droughts of tropical weather conditions. Adequate assistance from more fortunate areas in the world fails to arrive.[51] Instead, humans even add to the environmental crisis by their constant search for their own profit and benefit. We need

---

[48]Gould advocates the superiority of the "*bacillus*" to survive more than 3 miles underground, and also in the atmosphere at 150 degree celsius. *Bacilli* can survive under all circumstances. Their biochemy is incredibly diverse. The era of the *bacillus* coincides with all other eras. There have always been *bacilli* and there always will be! Similar views are presented by D. Quammen, *Het Lied van de Dodo, Eilandbiogeographie in een eeuw van extinctiess*, 1998, Amsterdam, 695p. The English original, *The Song of the Dodo* was published in the U.S.

[49]J. Blewett, "Social justice and creation spirituality." *The Way* (1989): 15.

[50]The Canadian William Rees has calculated that with a Western life-style everywhere, we would need 4 globes instead of one only. Given the number of people and the available space, a human could have 1.5 hectares at his/her disposal. Anno 1900 this was still 5.6. Today the Canadian uses 5 hectares, the US citizen 7.5. The Indian uses 0.4. With 3.5 hectares the Dutch need earthly space which is 15 times the size of their own country!

[51]One recent example: some islands in the Pacific Ocean which are right now threatened by the rise of the sea-level which is flooding the houses of the people, have unsuccessfully appealed to Australia for help.

only think here of the disasters of desertification, deforestation, salinization and waterlogging, destroying soil, converting fertile earth into barren land, and polluting earth, air, and water. Profit seeking agencies, however, remain deaf and qualify objections against their projects as "eco-fascism", a term invented to accuse the opponent of preferring force rather than reason to impose their ecological views and decisions.

Economy and Environment

Most governments take sides with the economists whenever environmentalists challenge their policies; those economists who believe that "whatever is unwise ecologically, is unwise economically too" are very few in number. Since the environmental world conferences in Rio de Janeiro (1992) and Kyoto (1997), the public opinion too has been increasingly confronted with the contrasting relationship between economy and environment. Robin Cook, foreign secretary of Great Britain, cites a recent report of the Intergovernmental Panel on Climatic Change (IPCC) which lists for the next century several dangers if a climatic change is not prevented: many more diseases in Latin America; acute water shortages in East Asia; 50% loss of wetlands at the North American coast. In the same period the CO_2 emission will double. No cooperation can be expected from the developing nations which themselves still need extensive economic growth. Are economy and environment mutually exclusive or mutually supportive? The issue may be briefly summarized as follows[52].

The environment feels threatened by economic growth. An increasing production causes a growing emission of CO_2 which pollutes the environment and leads to more sickness and death amongst all living organisms, including the human work force. Even a more efficient and clean use of energy — such as wind and solar power — in transport and industry cannot neutralize the pollution caused by economic growth. On the other hand, an economic growth is absolutely necessary because a slowing down of the economic growth leads to an increase in unemployment, loss of

---

[52]R. Mulder, "Niet milieu of economie maar milieu en economie," *Trouw* (27 September 1997).

income and purchasing-power, a loss also in competitive power in the industrial race between the bigger powers, such as USA, Japan, Europe, India, Brasil and China. Besides, most countries face national problems like a growing number of senior citizens, a mounting national debt, growing demands of national health, education and scientific research, expansion of transport, space programs, growing urbanization, worldwide military commitments, the ever more persistent cry for lower taxes.

Environmental care is yet one more challenge for any government. The fight against the greenhouse effect is only one aspect of this challenge. Can the economic growth and environmental care be both promoted and be even mutually beneficial, as some maintain? Or do they perhaps even need each other? Soil cleaning, measures for more environmental efficacy and less pollution, health care of the 'human capital', also promote economic progress. On the other hand, economic profit is required to finance the needed investments for the environmental care. The different viewpoints remain still far apart from each other. Where European governments aim at reducing greenhouse gas emissions, the USA government concentrates more on cleaner and less fossile fuels, and especially, new technologies.[53] Both would do well to move away from the dirty technologies of the past century towards the clean ones of the next century! Also, the USA government insists that in any policy strategy the developing countries must, along with the others, be involved.

Kyoto Compromise (1997)

Kyoto has reportedly arrived at a compromise. The reduction percentages to be realized between 2008 and 2012 will — with an average of 5.2% — be 6% for Japan, 7% for the USA, 8% for Europe. The involvement of developing nations has been left free but must be studied again and decided upon in the coming year. The

---

[53]Companies which see no possibilities to reduce their own emissions are suggested three alternate options: (1) trading emission rights with countries staying below their permitted percentage emissions. President Clinton suggests trading emission right between producers, utilizers, and investors; (2) voluntary contributions to afforestation; (3) subsidize modernizations of plants in developing nations.

proposal that developing countries such as China belongs too, would be asked to initiate voluntary reductions, and that countries with lower percentage emissions would be free to trade their surplus percentages with industrialized countries — obliged to reduce their own still exceeding percentage emissions —, met with strong resistance or severe suspicion. In a *Joint Implementation* it has been agreed that, through a transfer of technical know-how, the developing countries will be assisted in overcoming their problems of the greenhouse effect, among others, through the planting of numerous trees.

The position of China among the polluting nations is a matter of special concern because in the next century China will outstrip the USA which now, with 25% of all emissions, ranks first among the polluting countries, although it has only 5% of the world population. In the "dream-team" of the ten biggest polluters (all participants of the Kyoto Convention) are USA, China, Germany, Britain, Japan, Russia, Ukraine and India. Five of them are members of the club of G7, now G8, expected to lead the world into its economic paradise... Also, the fact that the closing session of Kyoto lasted 30 hours, clearly demonstrates how governments, politicians and industrial powers are fearing fierce competition and have become prisoners of their own possessions.

Nevertheless, we wish to end this survey of the Kyoto meeting on a positive note made by the scientist Benjamin Santer. In collaboration with 35 other scientists Santer evaluated and confirmed the thesis, supported by 65% of the American people, that *"very probably the humans are responsible for perceptible climatic changes on earth."* Kyoto went along with the conclusion and thus marked a historic event: *"humanity has become adult accepting the conclusion that global problems demand global solutions.*[54]*"*

---

[54]After Kyoto, Richard S. Lindzen, professor of metereology, wrote in the *Los Angeles Times* that at Kyoto the *Intergovernmental Forum for Climatic Change* failed to take away the scientific uncertainties about the causality between emissions and the greenhouse effect.

C. A sustainable development ever?

It will indeed be a long way to establish what is often called a "sustainable development." Such development does not only guarantee the rights of future generations but also respects the actual structures and practices of the society without doing harm to the environment or to people living in neighboring or other areas. Until that days arrives, sinister agencies will continue robbing the developing countries of their natural resources: gold and other minerals, wood, fisheries, animals, harvests, while unscrupulously dumping their wastes, polluting and harming the environment beyond repair. No one of them ever realizes that, with such behavior, even something of themselves is lost. For ever.

III.

STEWARDS OF CREATION

1. Divine Owner

The earth is the Lord's! The significance of this biblical vision has been masterly summarized by the Indian theologian Samuel Ryan. All earthly things clamor for their maker. This is not about rights and title but about God's ownership which for the earth is 'of the essence'. This vision is shared by both Muslims[55] and Christians. Some environmentalists go a step further by personalizing this ownership relation. More than some*thing*, the Earth is *Someone*, whom God loves, fashions, names, and ceaselessly overwhelms with gifts. And still more would happen to it when God's Kingdom would '*happen*' to it. In short: God makes history with the Earth.

Divine ownership is not one of power but of tender, caring love. God adorns his Earth over a period of millions of years in its evolution like a mother decks out her daughter, leading her on a pilgrimage through the three evolutionary phases of the material, the biological, and the cultural. The relationship deepens when the

---

[55]Hamzah Zeid: "wij moeten leren accepteren dat de natuur een deel van de schepping is en dus eigendom van God." in *De Islam en het vraagstuk van: Vrede, gerechtigheid en heelheid van de schepping* (Islam, 27), 4.

child Earth grows up and becomes God's Bride, embellished by Him with beauty and splendor, and graced with human warmth and clarity. The justice of the Earth becomes the foundation of God's own throne and reign (Is. 54, 13). Unfortunately, the avaricious human wickedness grabbed and took possession. A vain protest of the rainbow showed up in the sky. Nevertheless, *"let the Earth bring forth,"* the good and forgiving God of the Earth said. This makes the Earth also the Lord's self-manifestation, an unfolding of the Word of God. As human language cannot express this fittingly, silence becomes the better and cherished symbol.

The Earth is also God's Table where He invites and feeds us. "A feast of rich food"(Is. 25,6). Thanks to Our Father in Heaven and Our Mother on the Earth. This makes the Earth partner of the Covenant. The seasons of the Earth are the seasons of the Heart of God: loving, conceiving, brooding, warming, life-giving, and exploding into glory. Even the Book of Job ends in presenting creation as God's delight and radical grace. Art rather than consumption! Not so much to be used as to be contemplated.

Summing up: Divine ownership is not a smothering power but a generous presence. Likewise God's entire otherness enables Him to be an all-pervasive penetration. Different from everything else and hence creatively present in all. Isn't this an enthralling echo of the surprising and beautiful Buddhist vision: the Earth as Brahman's *leela*, God's play?

2.   Human Steward

Next, the Earth is ours. Given to us by God. Given to the whole of God's family to serve the needs and creative talents of everyone. Our relationship to the earth is in the shape of work, food, knowledge, contemplation, gift-giving. The Earth is the "Common Body of Humanity." But the Earth is not to be taken for granted, neither is she dead, nor to be used only. We must celebrate her, and in her celebrate God.

A very supportive worldview is formulated by Mansukh Patel[56], a hindu from Kenya who, after his education in England and a brief spell in a desert, decided to spend the rest of his life serving humanity as a catalyst. Always sleeping outside on the ground, Mansukh pleads for taking root in the earth, just as trees do. "*Nature is my second mother*", says Mansukh. Without a link with mother Earth people shut their heart and lose their humanity. They cannot care properly for the Earth and its inhabitants with real and sincere compassion. From there on the appropriating, exploiting and ill-treating of Mother Earth takes over. Humans start consuming only to fill their empty hearts. For the Church Fathers private ownership is nothing less than idolatry[57]. For them, ownership is avarice, violence, deprivation, capturing spoils of war, thievery, and the root cause of discord, conflicts and wars. It contradicts the purposes of God written into the fabric of the Earth!

Mansukh Patel's final observation concerns religions. World religions must radiate and stimulate unity. They are challenged to mutually accept each other: each following their own path towards the Divine. The Divine is present in all cultures. Every time in another culture, someone stands up who is able to convey truths to others: 5000 years ago Krishna did so in North India; 2600 years ago Siddhattha Buddha Gotama came, followed by Jesus Christ 2000 years ago; 600 years later the Prophet Moḥammad Ibn Abdallah proclaimed Allah's Message, followed by Francis of Assisi again 600 years later, and once more 700 years later by the modern messiah

---

[56]See P.Wessels, Mansukh Patel: "Nature is my second mother," *BIJEEN* XXXI (1998): 7-13. Patel recommends becoming a vegetarian to practice compassion towards animals.

[57]F.J. Hinkelammert, in his theology of the economy, elaborates a liberation theology which breaks away from "*the service of the idols of death*" which takes place when the production of riches leads to the poverty of the masses. This idolatry manifests itself on the scale of values if the exchange-value is given priority over the use-value. Economy becomes then a value in itself. He criticizes the ideology which believes in the realization of the Utopia through an increased production which by itself will supposedly put an end to all scarcity of goods. Hinkelmann never tires of repeating that the liberal market leads instead to poverty because it produces only goods which will benefit those with financial power to buy. The root cause is the desire to produce goods which can be bought, instead of producing goods which enable people to live.

Mohandas Karamchand (Mahatma) Gandhi, who said about our utilizing the earth: *"there is enough for everyone's need, never enough for anyone's greed."* Mansukh admires Francis of Assisi 'who lived close to nature and preached simplicity'. He concludes his conversation with Patricia Wessels proclaiming *"Love is the best cement of the world, joining cultures to religion, and turning enemies into friends."*

IV.

FRANCISCAN ECOLOGY

1. Theological Foundation

Francis, Fishes, Flowers?

St. Francis of Assisi is frequently painted and sculptured in the company of flowers, fishes and birds. He soon gained popularity as the lover of trees and animals; a relationship which gradually extended to the whole universe because of his well known *Canticle of all Creatures*. In 1979 the present Pope, John Paul II, proclaimed him patron of Ecology. For this and other reasons, throughout the Christian world, Francis has become one of the most popular saints and mystics of young and old, Catholic and otherwise.

This 'sweet', attractive presentation, however, has overshadowed the more important content of Francis' message and his commitment to the reform of church and world. The 'brotherly and sisterly' cats and dogs, blessed on World Animal Day — Francis' birthday! — have lost their original setting in which the Franciscan Ecology should have placed them.

Francis, lover of poverty?

Francis suffers still another misunderstanding which sidetracked his basic inspiration and spirituality. At an early stage of people's admiration for Francis he was given the title "Il Poverello." It happened in the transition from ancient feudalism to medieval capitalism[58], when many powerless people found themselves reduced to dire poverty and forced to roam streets begging for food, medicines, and shelter for the night. Out of mercy and solidarity Francis apparently joined them and extolled an evangelical lifestyle of poverty. No wonder, therefore, his admirers say, that in his definitive Rule of Life Francis speaks mystically of the "Highest Poverty,"[59] as if poverty is a blessing to be sought after, and not an evil to be fought against!

Francis' Fundamental Option

Nothing is farther from the truth. Instead, Francis protested against and condemned poverty wholeheartedly. Francis' fundamental option was his intuition that the root of all evil, including poverty, was the human craving for ownership, the unquenchable thirst to have and always have more property. Hence Francis' conviction that Adam's first sin was in fact one of appropriation. Adam wants independence and "exalts" himself to 'lord' instead of recognizing God's Lordship. Being Lord is claiming ownership and the right to dispose of what is really property of God. The utopia of paradise is destroyed by Adam's own will[60] because all things are created and presented to us as gifts of the Lord. Gifts, which have to be appreciated, respected, used and, at the appropriated time, returned to the Owner Creator of all things.[61]

---

[58]In his critique on religion and science, Sadiq Al-Azam, professor at the Damascus University, wishes to inform the West about the political and social thought in the Islamic world. The advice he gives to Muslims not to be self-complacent, is equally valid for Christians. Self-criticism can do a lot of good to both, all the more now that neither religion has any means of power at its disposal. Fundamentalist movements do not constitute, according to Sadiq Al-Azam, any real threat to anybody.

[59]"*Nor should they feel ashamed since the Lord made himself poor for us in this world. This is the summit of highest poverty.*" Rule of 1223, VI.

[60]"For the person eats of the tree (=sins)...who appropriates to himself his own will..." Adm. II, 3.

[61]Parallel or relevant texts are: Adm. IV; Rule of 1221. VII, 10 and 14; XVII, 4; Rule of 1223, VI, 1 and 2; Adm.VII, 4; VIII, 3; XIX, 1;XXII, 2.

Against property and appropriation

'The thrust of Francis' intuition is not a promotion of or option for poverty but a strong opposition to the most radical form of any property and appropriation. This choice is the fruit of personal experience in a family and city which got carried away by newly discovered sources of income. Through success and failure, vastly different levels of rich and poor people came into being. To examine his position and strengthen the newly found style of life for himself and his first followers, Francis set out to find back the original order of justice and harmony. This loving hunt for the utopia of the first paradise opened his eyes for the excluding and dividing effect of appropriation and ownership. The continuous search-for-more resulted in a growing conflict not only within his family, but also with his beloved birthplace of Assisi. Like other centers, it became addicted to the new economy. Finally the Church itself became deeply involved in wars to snatch the Land of Jesus from the hands of the Sultan. Francis chose another way to utopia: his program aimed at removing the root cause of friction, i.e., ownership, and instead approach the other (whomever) not by lording it over but instead by willing to serve as the lesser one. Francis' ambition was his dream of an alternate society of peace: a Brotherhood of followers which bans the root cause of evil definitively out of its midst.[62]

Scriptural Foundation

Francis found in the Scriptures the needed confirmation of his option of life. They clearly stated that All Good comes from God, maker and owner of all things. Francis' Brotherhood is intended to replace the evil society founded by Adam who — in the words of Francis — himself was the first one to fall into the trap of

---

[62] J. Hoeberichts, *Franciscus en de Islam*, 35-104. (trad. *Francis and Islam*, 61-134). In the 14th century a group of Francis' followers, called Spirituals, taught that neither Christ nor the apostles possessed anything. Pope John XXII reacted and accused the friars of being arrogant to reject ownership as well as beoming more acquisitive than any other mendicant order. The friars responded by calling the pope heretical. Thereupon the emperor, Louis of Bavaria, elected the anit-pope, Nicholas V in 1328.

ownership. In his second admonition Francis writes: *"For the person eats of the tree of the knowledge of good who appropriates to himself his own will and thus exalts himself over the good things which the Lord says and does in him."* Francis was radical in his views in whatever shape or form. Inspired by St. Paul's *"just as sin came into the world through one human, and death came through sin, and so death spread to all because all have sinned...Therefore, just as one human's trespass led to the condemnation of all..."* (Rom.5, 12 and 18), Francis sees in Adam's sin of appropriation the downfall of all creation. Similarly, the new utopian family too includes all creation: each and everyone, reaching out to animals, flowers, and all things created. An all inclusive Brotherhood indeed!

3.   Franciscan Ecology

The theological interpretation of his life provided Francis with a comprehensive vision of God as Creator and Owner, and a radical dependence on God. The humans must truly and lovingly care for God's gift and share it with all other creatures. All creation is a temporary gift, 'on loan' as it were, in due time to be returned to the Divine Giver. These foundational principles show us the direction of a Franciscan Ecology.

Goal

Franciscan Ecology chooses as its principal goal: to convince humans that God is Lord and Owner of the Universe; humans are only stewards and equals of other creatures. Franciscans listen to the call of the Earth for its rightful place among all other creatures[63]. The present sinful claim of the humans for unlimited ownership, and their unquenchable thirst for ever more, is the root cause of all evil and could lead to the ultimate destruction of the entire Universe.

Objectives

- Franciscan ecology proclaims God's Lordship of all creation and denounces the present claim to ownership by humans as sinful, dangerous, and destructive.

---

[63]Blewett, 15.

- Franciscan ecology challenges humanity to assume steward-ship to govern and administer, and all humans to assume it *jointly*, together with the obligation to real accountability.
- Franciscan ecology maintains that respect for creation includes the fair, and — to the extent possible — the equal distribution of Mother Earth, all means of living, and enough potentiality of development for all.
- Franciscan ecology warns the humans that the Earth is not just dirt to walk on but a sacred entity to be recognized as a "single, living, self-regulating organism". *(Gaia)*
- Franciscan ecology supports the preservation of nature, also for the sake of joy, beauty and health of all living creatures.

Strategies

- Franciscan ecology, rejecting individualistic visions, deals with the Universe respectfully, i.e., as a united whole, "car-rying a dignity and a mirroring of the Divine"[64], in which our faith recognizes the hand of God, and of which the hu-man Jesus is the crowning moment.
- Franciscan ecology proclaims the interconnectedness of all creatures in a shared life through common origin and com-mon destination. Humans are invited to explore, respect, support, and explain to others the manifold connections be-tween the countless creatures.[65]
- Franciscan ecology views the interconnectedness of all creatures as the basis of a fraternal and sisterly bond be-tween all creatures, which results in a resolve to work for a family spirit of mutual interest, respect, care, and affection, instead of claiming ownership.
- Franciscan ecology recognizes this family bond as founda-tional for global responsibility which implies that:

  1. we plead and work for a proper balance between global and regional structures;

---

[64]Blewett, 13.
[65]Blewett, 15.

2. the world needs a global population policy including each and every individual;
3. borders must be geographic and functional, instead of national or political;
4. a second worldwide language next to the mother tongue is recommended;
5. a worldwide accessibility of all channels of formation and information be guaranteed;
6. a global responsibility for and availability of clean earth, water and air be put in place;[66]
7. any global economy at the expense of any sister or brother is to be corrected.

- Franciscan ecology urges to include in the "option of the poor" the endangered species, strip-mined hills, eroded croplands, polluted rivers, acidified lakes, and gutted mountains[67] and therefore promotes a worldwide combat against any form of pollution of air, water, and earth.
- Franciscan ecology will work for a selfless stewardship and a joint responsibility for everything without which there can be no hope for a future of things, plants, animals,[68] and humans.[69] Franciscans wonder whether people are aware that they truly harm themselves by ill-treating Mother Earth, ripping, raping, robbing, oppressing, despising, and discarding her.[70]

---

[66]500 Franciscan sisters and brothers in Ho Chi Minh City, Vietnam, plead in a document, entitled *Mother Earth*, on the environment for *"safe water, rural roads and bridges, tree planting, small scale irrigation works, rehabilitation of virgin lands and resettlement schemes."* In *Information* X (MZF, Bonn, Germany, 1997).

[67]Blewett, 17.

[68]Many people are asking for guidance in problems of the bio-industry: medical experimentation, cloning, intensified rearing and breading, cross-breeding, etc. Opponents of the present lawless situation speak of another 'holocaust.' They also point a finger at the Church and blame Religions in general.

[69]Two examples may suffice to make the point: rainforests are essential for supplying oxygen to the lungs of humans and animals. A certain kind of flowers have kept our forefather-apes alive.

[70]Blewett, 20.

- Franciscan ecology promotes a peace which is the fruit of justice and "even more the fruit of the right order between humans and the Earth." Earth is a peace-institute teaching co-operation, co-ordination, patience, and searching, one species linked, in life and death fashion, to another, so that, all along the way, life might perdure.[71]
- Franciscan ecology seconds any effort to preserve nature, also for the sake of joy, beauty and health of all living creatures.
- Franciscan ecology supports a global strategy to combat any crime against creation.

CONCLUSION

RAYS OF HOPE

Dialog between rich and poor on "enough"

The purpose of this article has been to question the ethical validity of ownership, to nail the evil consequences of appropriation, to replace it with responsible stewardship of God's creation, and its indispensable counterpart accountability. These principles could open the way to a sustainable development with an economy of the sufficient, instead of pursuing an ever-increasing acquisition of more. The former offers at least a real chance that in future there will be enough for everyone to live. The 'rat race' for always more wealth, more money, and more power, on the contrary, will lead to an inescapable and disastrous conflict, and possibly even to the ultimate destruction.

Therefore, rich and poor must come out of their hiding-places and ghettos and meet each other.[72] They are the interested parties

---

[71]Blewett, 22.

[72]An inspiring example of collaboration has been started by Mr. Muhammed Yunus in Bangladesh who invented the system of *"micro-credits,"* that is, small loans of 50 or 100 dollars to poor people to be paid back within 6 months. With that money they can free themselves from the clutches of greedy moneylenders, or start their own small business. Experience shows that 90% pays back within the

to discuss ways and means to arrive at a more just notion of ownership and accountability in the future society. Religions, on their part, must urge[73] their rich members to better serve the Common Good of society. This call will meet with much resistance, because the majority's conviction and experience point in the opposite direction. Private ownership and economic success are growing rapidly in the Western World. At the same time God and Religion in the West are becoming ever more irrelevant. Therewith, the gap between believer and non-believer is ever widening. This secularizing process makes a general disaster ever more likely to happen.

Not all is lost

Fortunately, this article need not, unavoidably, end on a negative note. There are several pointers to a sustainable economy which offers better chances for a society in which citizens can live in real justice and true peace. Facts and figures must dialog with values of solidarity and mercy. The "Sabbath" in the meaning of <*taking distance from*> can create enough space to resist the dominant craving for profit and wealth. Three avenues come into view which point to future orientations of new and better goals, objectives and strategies for a healthy economy and a respected and enjoyable environment.

1.   Coalescing Non-profit Organizations

In a recent interview Prof. R. Lubbers[74] calls globalization the result of political, economic and technical developments and is

---

stipulated period. Yunes' Bank today, 20 years later, has 2.1 million customers in 36,000 villages in Bangladesh. Worldwide the project serves about 13 million people. The target for the year 2005 is to reach 100 million people. The World Bank has contributed 200 million dollars to the project of which Hillary Rodham Clinton has assumed patronage. A Franciscan in Vietnam, Jean Francois Nguyen Gia Thinh, inspired by the success of Muhammed Yunus, has started a similar project with the help of CIDSE (international), BILANCE (Dutch) and CARITAS CISTERCIENSIS WESTMALLE (Belgium). See *The Pelgrim* IX (1998): 15.

[73]Christians would prefer to use the term "*evangelize*".

[74]Prof. Ruud Lubbers, an economist by profession, was the Duth Minister of Economic Affairs for four years. He then became the Prime Minister of the Netherlands for 12 years. After his 20 years in political service, Lubbers returned to

there to stay[75]. The world will have to come to terms with this phenomenon which by itself is neither good nor bad. We are witnessing the birth of a world market, worldwide communications, and a general desire towards democratic government. The option for a multiple joint strategy against (1) the discriminating exclusion of peoples and individuals, (2) the outdated dominance of nationalistic governments and (3) ruthless monopolies of multinationals, provides opportunities for voluntary workers, non-governmental organizations, and unpaid labor, while calling for fresh initiatives of individuals and organizations, like Green Peace, Amnesty International, *"Os Sem Terra"*, like-minded feminist movements, etc. They all are non-profit agencies in the civil society which opt for human values with a positive influence on governments, feudal landlords and industry. They could link up with national and international consumer lobbies, labor organizations watching salaries and working conditions, approach international bodies like I.L.O., the European Union, etc. Together they should engage these powerful bodies in dialogue, organize actions, exert pressure. All of them together can plead for "ethical consumerism", "social accounting", "codes of conduct" drafted by the companies themselves, "taxes on foreign exchange transactions", the rights of weaker[76] sections in society, and warn against a one-sided economy which ignores the rights and the advantages of an environmental policy. Only then can we hope for a balance between local and global, between economy and environment, between secular and religious values, between action and contemplation.

---

the non-governmental section of society as a resource person for NGO's. Presently he is professor of 'Globalisation' at the Universities of Brabant, the Netherlands, and at Harvard University in the United States. As of January 1, 2000, he is President of the World Wildlife Fund (W.W.F.), member of the Earth Council, and the Independent World Commission of the Oceans. He is also president of the T.N.O. (Applied Technology of Natural Science Research).

[75]In *One World, Ready or Not*, W. Greider compares globalization with a vehicle with very capable passengers on board but with no one at the wheel! Or as Birkin asks: *"once everyone has everything: what next?"*

[76]Pope John Paul II to the Pont.Acad.Soc.Sciences in April 1997: *"The more global the market, the more it must be balanced by a global culture of solidarity, attentive to the needs of the weakest."* Cited by Vallely & Linden, 1035.

2. Dialogue between Economy and Religion

Ruud Lubbers puts on record a growing conviction that economists and religions should meet and initiate a common search for new solutions. We can report two efforts in this direction. The first one is a recent address of Rev. Bryan Hehir[77] to Mr. Camdessus, Managing Director, and his staff of the International Monetary Fund (I.M.F.), held on May 30th 1997, in Washington, DC, in the presence of 35 members of the Religious Working Group on the roles of the World Bank and the I.M.F. Usually the I.M.F. and religious/missioners are poles apart: the former concerns itself with economics, the latter with the religious life of the people. Yet, differences need not and should not lead to irreconcilable oppositions. Hehir takes up the challenge to build bridges, because he has noticed a mutual readiness to listen. He begins his talk referring to voices and visions which humans all have and which they trust. At the institutional level, there is an I.M.F. vision which says: "Globalization has transformed markets into a stern and impatient master." This at times unyielding vision points to the logic of the market in its macro dimension. The missioners hear other stern voices: those of the Old Testament prophets, Matthew's Gospel (ch. 25), and Francis of Assisi in the Middle Ages, which tell us that God is with and loves the poor.[78] Missioners have experiences with hungry and dying children, and are ready to give 'the last change in their pocket' although they hail from the rich West. Such experiences Jesus has laid down in his stories and parables. How, then, do we, in our multiple visions, put together the logic of laws with the logic of stories? The truth is not on one side only. We recognize the wisdom of reason and experience how to run an economy, but we also listen to the visions of prophets and the experience of missioners. Both poles have a common end and purpose: *the human development.*

---

[77]The following information is taken from notes of a meeting between the Director and staff members of the I.M.F., and a Religious Working Group in Washington, DC, on May 30, 1997.

[78]At the recent conference of all US Mayors in December 1997, official information was given that in the course of 1997 the number of people living below the poverty line, has increased by 16%!

Another effort is the encounter between Economy and Religion convened jointly by James Wolfensohn, President of the World Bank, and George Carey, Archbishop of Canterbury, Anglican Church, on February 18-19, 1998, in Lambeth Palace, headquarters of the Anglicans in London. This two days' symposium on *"Poverty in the World"* has been attended by nine leaders of world religions, among whom *Anglicans, Orthodox* (Metrop. Johannes of Pergamom [Constantinople] and Archim. Feofan [Moscow], *Lutherans* (Bishop Th. O. Laiser of Tanzania), *Muslims* (crown prince El-Hassan of Jordan, the Aga Khan, and Dr. Mustafa Ceric of Bosnia), *Catholics* (Card. R. Etchegaray and his deputy Mgr. D. Martin), *Jews* (the American Rabbi A. Hertzberg (cons.), former Chief Rabbi of France, René Sirat [orth.]) and Dr. Th. Lachs (liberal), *Hindus* (Swami Vibudhesha Teertha of South India and Achaya Srivatsa Goswami), *Buddhists* (Nambaryn Enkhbayar of Mongolia and the social activist and monk Sulak Sivaraksa of Thailand, some *Taoists, Sikhs, Jinus,* and members of the the *Bahá'i Community.* The thirty some participants — including three women — discussed ways towards better mutual understanding and joint action against world poverty and hunger, care of the environment, preservation of the cultural heritage, sacred places, and social services. An important priority will be to better integrate the values of culture, religion, and social structures into the development strategy. The World Bank invited the religious authorities to collaborate in the writing of the annual reports of the Bank. This recent consultation resulted in the opening of a new channel of dialogue which was baptized *"The World Faiths Development Dialogue."*[79]

4. Joint Approach of World Religions

Muslims and Christians alike have started talking with each other more frequently than they used to. In a common consultation, in 1996, 37 delegates from ten different countries recognized the fact of "Two Faiths, one God" in the command of both Jesus and

---

[79]See also "World Bank meets religious groups for aid summit," *The Tablet* (28 February, 1998): 295.

Mohammad to see their service to the neighbor as a service to God[80].

They welcome growing prosperity and technological progress as improvements of the quality of life. They disapprove that prices of commodities are controlled by market forces distant from peoples' lives. Next, they worry about the increasing number of people below the poverty line, the exploitation of women, children, migrant workers, indigenous people and the *dalits*. Then, they regret that 'wealth' is reserved for a privileged few. Further, economic speculation is rejected as a new and dangerous type of gambling. They also qualify the ecological destruction as an outright offense of the Creator which hurts especially those who have a "fragile relationship with nature." Finally, they urge, Muslims and Christians must rigorously analyze "religious, historical, social, cultural, economic, political" dimensions of society in order to propose concrete improvements.

The Utopian Vision of Luke 2, 14.

These recent phenomena should encourage voluntary non-profit organizations, economic institutions and world religions, among them surely Islam and Christianity, to jointly study ways and means to balance God's Supreme Ownership and Humans' Responsible Stewardship of all created things[81]. An agreed upon balance between

---

[80]Religious experts are hereby invited to write a *Grammar of Coexistence*, H. Kissinger's term to describe Rabin's political life-work of building peace with the Palestinians who in 1995 was slain by a fellow Israelite!

[81]The Secular Franciscans of Italy published a document *"Forgive poor countries their debts"* and motivate their plea referring to the fatal consequences of an everlasting cycle of loans, interests and repayments. In the same document they also demand that (1) two commissions be established: (a) an inter-governmental one and (b) another one of non-governmental organizations both of which must collect data on how governments, suspected of unlawful appropriations, assign and utilize the loans; (2) wide-spread and repeated violations against the Right of Development must be listed amongst the "crimes against humanity", and be prosecuted by the International Court of Justice. Thirdly, they ask the Security Council for a special session of the Council to investigate, on the one hand, how governments of the South have administered these development funds, and, on the other hand, how the authorities of the North have assigned and actually utilized these public funds for Development Funds (reported in *Fraternitas*, nr. 29 February, 1998; German edition).

Divine Ownership and Human Stewardship will be the bridge towards the Third Millennium with a well-established equilibrium between a just economy and a healthy environment. *"Out of an economic and ecological **apartheid** no common future will ever emerge. Apartheid must first be removed.*[82]*"* Only then will the road lie open for the journey towards Utopia: the Kingdom of God on Earth in which there will be *"Glory to God and Peace to all Peoples."*

BIBLIOGRAPHY

Armstrong, K., *Muhammed, a western attempt to understand Islam.* London,1991.

Balasuriya, T. "For sanity." in *Jeevadhara* XXV (1995)nr.147,191-218.

Barry, T., *The dream of the earth.* 1988.

Bavel, T.J.van, "De grenzen van eigendom bij Augustinus," *Franciscaans Leven* LXXIX (1996): 59-69.

Birch, Ch. and Cobb, J.B., *The Liberation of life.*

Blewett, J., "Social justice and creation spirituality." *The Way* (1989): 13-16.

Boersema, J. J., *Thora en Stoa over mens en natuur. Een bijdrage aan het milieudebat over duurzaamheid en kwaliteit.* Groningen, 1997.

Borgman, E. "Franz J. Hinkelammert: kritiek op dienst aan de afgoden van de dood, in de naam van de God van het leven." *Riding the Juggernaut* (1996) 25-30.

Brinkman, J. "The Kyoto Environment Conference from a Catholic Perspective." *The Japan Mission Journal* LII nr.1 Spring (1998): 3-11.

Brown, L. a.o. *State of the World. A world watch Institute Report on Progress Toward a Sustainable Society,* New York/London.

Butselaar, J.v. a.o. *Gerechtigheid en Barmhartigheid. Mogelijkheden en grenzen van ontwikkelingssamenwerking.* Kampen, 1989.

Carrier, H. *The social doctrine of the Church revisited,* Vatican City.

---

[82]V. Shiva, *De armoedige...* 118.

Colijn, K. and Rusman, P., "De metamorfose van de moderne staat; interview with Suzan Strabge." *Vrij Nederland* LVIII (1997): 22-24.

Cullinan, T. "The politics of ownership." *The Month* (1995): 11-15.

Daly, H.E. "Towards some operational principles of sustainable development." *Ecological Economics* II (1990): 1-6.

Daly, H.E. and Cobb, J., *For the common good, redirecting the economy towards community, the environment and a sustainable future.* Boston, 1989.

Daly, H.E. and K. Towsend. *Valuing the earth. Ecology, economics, ethics.* Cambridge MA, 1993.

Directory of Environmental Activities and Resources in the North American Religious Community, in La Croix, J., *Environmental Resource Book* (Rome: Franciscan Office for Justice, Peace and Ecology, 1993) 132-157.

Dieren, W.van. "De kern van het millieuconflict." *Hervormd Nederland* LI (1995): 12-15.

Doornik, N.van. *Franciscus van Assisi. Een profeet voor onze tijd.* Hilversum, 1973.

Doyle, E. *St. Francis and the song of brotherhood and sisterhood.* St. Bonaventure, New York: The Franciscan Institute, 1997.

Driessen, H., a.o. *In het huis van de Islam.* Nijmegen, 1997.

Duchrow, U. "God or Mammon: economics in conflict." *Mission Studies* XIII (1996): 32-67.

Economic Justice for all, Pastoral letter USA Bishops. Washington, DC: US Catholic Conference, 1986.

Economische gerechtigheid, een bundel verhandelingen en ervaringen over armoede, commissie justitia et pax, Nederland, 1995.

Een wereld van verschil. Nieuwe kaders voor ontwikkelingssamenwerking in de jaren negentig, Beleidsnota, Den Haag, 1990.

Flood, D. *Work for everyone, Francis of Assisi and the ethic of service.* Quezon City, 1997.

—. *Francis of Assisi and the Franciscan Movement.* Quezon City, 1989.

Forrester. V. *De terreur van de economie.* Ambo, 1997.

Fox, F. "Rich man, poor man." *The Tablet* (4 October 1997): 1253.

Francis and Clare: *The Complete Works*, translation and introduction by R. J. Armstrong, and I. Brady. New York: Paulist Press, 1982.

Goudzwaard, B. *Voor niets gaat de zon op.* Merwede, 1989.

Goudzwaard, B. a.o., *Gerechtigheid en Barmhartigheid,* ICCO, Kok,Kampen, 1989.

Goudzwaard, B and Lange, H. de, *Genoeg van te veel, Genoeg van te weinig.Wissels omzetten in de Economie.* Ten Have, Baarn, 1986.

Gould, S.J. *Full House,* 1997.

Grond, A. *Moeder Natuur en haar recalcitrante dochters. Een feministische stem in het milieudebat,* J.v.Arkel, Utrecht, 1998.

Harries, R. "Forgive them their debts." *The Tablet* (20 September 1997): 118–1182.

Haught, J.F. "The emergent environment and the problem of cosmic purpose." *Environmental Ethics* VIII (1986).

——. *The cosmic adventure.* New York, 1984.

——. *Ecology, cosmology and theology; a triology.* Woodstock Report, June, 1994.

Hoeberichts, J. *Franciscus en de Islam,* Assen,1994.

——. *Francis and the Islam.* Quincy, 1997.

——. "The second admonition," Newsletter OFM Pakistan, 1981, *Francis the Peacemaker,* Vol. 1 (1994) 40-46.

——. "Francis and his option for the poor from a Liberation-theological perspective." *Franciscan Digest* VI (1996): 27-43.

Hoogstraten, H.D.van. "Geld en Geest. *Over milieuethiek,* Baarn, 1993.

Hug, J. "Social responsibility in the age of globalization," *Center Focus* 136 (May 1997) 1-2.

Human Development Report 1996. For the United Nations Development Program (UNDP). Oxford University Press, 1996.

Isamu, A. "Environmental Crisis and the Transformation of Creation" *The Japan Mission Journal* LII, no.1 (Spring 1998): 12-25.

Küng, H. and J. Moltmann. "Islam challenge for Christianity," *Concilium,* 1994.

Leeuwen, B.van, *Armoede als Franciscaanse levensweg nu,* Utrecht, s.d., 7-24.

——. "Armoede bij Franciscus als recht van de armen." *Franciscaans Leven* LX (1977): 202-222.

Leeuwen, P.van and Verheij, S., "Het kwaad van de eigen wil." In *Woorden van heil van een kleine mens, reeks commentaren op de Franciscaanse bronnen.* Utrecht, 24-29.

McDonagh, S. *To care for the earth. A call to a new theology.* England, 1986.

McFague, S. *Models of God, theology for an ecological, nuclear age.* Philadelphia, 1987.

—. *Moral imperatives for addressing structural adjustment and economic reforms measures.* Religious working group on the World Bank and the IMF. *Maryknoll Peace and Justice*, May 1997.

Mulder, R. "Niet milieu of economie maar milieu en economie," *Trouw* (27 September 1997).

Munster, H.van *Een steen in de vijver, vrede en gerechtigheid na 'de dood van Marx'.* Kampen, 1993.

—. *De Celestijnse belofte, uitdaging of belofte?* 1996. Overdruk uit Benedictijns Tijdschrift, 1996.

—. "Een rijke heeft het moeilijk," *Commissie Justitia et Pax Nederland*, Nr.12, Oegstgeest, 1997.

—. "Aan alles hangt een prijskaartje." *Franciscaans Leven* LXXIX (1996): 78-92.

Neem tijd om te leven, Actie tegen de 24-uurseconomie, Interkerkelijk Contact in Overheidszaken (CIO). February, 1998.

Nolthenius, H., *Een man uit het dal van Spoleto.* Amsterdam, 1988.

Noordergraaf, H., "Ulrich Duchrow: Een belijdende Kerk in verzet tegen het mondiale kapitalisme." *Riding the Juggernaut* 31-34.

Pirkl, M., a.o., *One Earth, one world, one heart. Preparing for the next millennium.* A resource collection for Franciscans. Washington, DC: The Franciscan Federation, 1994.

Prisma van de Islam, begrippen van A tot Z. Utrecht, 1995.

Pronk, J. *De kritische grens. Beschouwingen over tweespalt en orde.* Amsterdam, 1994.

Quammen, D. *Het Lied van de dodo.Eilandbiogeographie in een eeuw van extincties.* Amsterdam: Atlas, 1998.

Rayan, S. "The earth is the Lord's," *Vidyajyoti Journal of Theological Reflection* LIV (1990): 113-132.

Rees, W. *Our Ecological Footprint. s.d.*

Robert, P. *The issue of dehumanizing poverty in the Indian Subcontinent. An Islamic and Catholic perspective,* 2 vols. 1997.

Rolston, H. *Science and religion.* New York, 1987.

Salemink, T. "Michael Novak: katholieke legitimatie van de vrije markt." *Riding the Juggernaut, Het debat over theologie en economie,* (1996) 73-77.

Scheltens, D. "Toeëigening en onteigening." *Franciscaans Leven* LXXIX (1996): 51-58.

Sevenhoven, H. "Leven zonder eigendom. Over het 'eigene' van de eerste minderbroeders." *Franciscaans Leven* LXXIX (1996): 70-77.

Shiva V. a.o. *De armoedige levensvisie van het Rijke Westen. Milieu en Derde Wereldproblemen: het resultaat van geestelijke monocultuur,* Baarn, 1997.

Shiva V. "Wil je meer, neem dan minder." *De Bazuin* LXXX (1997): 12-13.

Shomanah, M.W. Dube. "Praying the Lord's Prayer in a Global Economic Era." *The Ecumenical Review* IL (1997): 439-450.

Social and ethical aspects of Economics. A colloquium in the Vatican, Vatican City, 1992.

Te doen gerechtigheid. Zeven overwegingen over de christelijke vormgeving van een rechtvaardige sociale rechtvaardigheid voor iedereen, Commissie justitia et pax. Nederland, 1995.

Vallely, P. and I. Linden. "The Tide can be tamed. Doing battle with globalization." *The Tablet* (16 August 1997) 1034-5.

Verhelst, T. *Het recht anders te zijn,* Antwerpen.

Vischer, L. "Climate Change, Sustainability and Christian Witness." *The Ecumenical Review* 49 (1997):142-161.

Waardenburg, J. a.o. *Islam. Norm en werkelijkheid,* Antwerpen, 1984.

Wal, J. v.d. *De woekeraar en de graanboer,* UTP-section 18, 1996.

Wessels, P. "Mansukh Patel: De natuur is mijn tweede moeder" ["Nature is my second mother"]." *BIJEEN* XXXI (1998): 7-13.

Wielenga, B. "Biblical reasons for resistance against the sway of capital." *Vidyajyoti Journal of Theological Reflection* LX (1996): 45-58.

Zeid Kailani, Hamzah, *De Islam en het vraagstuk van: Vrede, gerechtigheid en heelheid van de schepping.* Islam, 27.

—. *Islamitische visie op vrede, gerechtigheid en respect voor de schepping,* Address on Peace and Justice (*pro manuscripto*).

Zwaenenpoel, P.P., "Culture and the Globalization of the Economy." *EUNTES-DIGEST* XXXI (1998): 17-26.